IN SEARCH OF CHRIST

For my family –
with deep affection

James O'Halloran SDB

In Search of Christ
A PRAYER BOOK FOR SEEKERS

COLUMBA

First published in 2004 by
THE COLUMBA PRESS
55A Spruce Avenue, Stillorgan Industrial Park, Blackrock,
Co Dublin, Ireland

Cover by Bill Bolger
Cover picture by Anne Fitzgerald
Origination by The Columba Press
Printed in Ireland by ColourBooks Ltd, Dublin

ISBN 1 85607 452 8

A Jesus Prayer

Jesus you are
the lonesome cloud
  sailing celestial seas,
artist fashioning wide sky
  of radiant vermilion,
a distant star
  pulsing emerald, saphire, gold,
the gleaming dove
  tumbling in gentle air,
o'erweening Everest,
Pacific phosphorescent.

Jesus you are
the hug
  of true friend,
the fair curl
  on brow of drowsy child,
the prisoner
  in lonely cell
  waiting
  painfully,
the shaggy busker
  twanging his guitar
  to heedless crowds
  on city street,
pinch-faced mother
  with babe in flimsy shawl
  begging for loose change
  upon O'Connell Bridge,
her fashion-plate sister too
  gliding blithely by
  unthinkingly.

Jesus you are
the hand that soothes
   the fevered brow
   of AIDS,
soldier lowering rifle
   to spare the life
   of cowering foe
   on poppied field.

Jesus, in a word
your name is
Love -
love that smiles
love that weeps
love that never fails.

(James O'Halloran)

Contents

ENDINGS
– and New Dawn

Introduction

This is a prayer book for people who are searching for Christ. They may be doing so because, historically, they consider him one of the greatest religious leaders of all time. They may be doing so because they come from a Christian tradition and want to take a fresh look at this person for themselves. They may be intrigued by his message of universal and unconditional love. Or, indeed, they may be amazed at the claim made that he is divine as well as human – the Son of God in fact, born of the Virgin Mary. Because of this latter claim, many may feel tempted to immediately dismiss him and his followers as charlatans. Yet, without giving him and his message a fair hearing, this is hardly rational.

God is infinitely beyond grasping by our reason. Yet God's existence does not contradict reason. We cannot put God under a microscope, but neither can we put love under a microscope and there is no doubting the existence of love. I myself look into the heart of a flower and, for me, all that is transcendent becomes possible. I know there are people for whom this is sincerely not so.

The Christian and Jewish scriptures tell us that God is infinitely beyond our comprehension. Which does not mean that we cannot know anything about God, only that, no matter how much we know, there is still infinitely more to learn. Paradoxically, the same scriptures inform us that God is near us, even within us. A great mystery. Whether near or far, the Lord of Creation is beyond our poor powers. Because of this, I believe that ultimately the only way that God could truly have made contact with us was to become one of us. And this is what happened through Christ.

These mysteries are obviously outside the field of strict science which deals in observable data. Yet there is a whole world beyond observable data, and many scientists of integrity do not deny this. They in fact point out that this is the realm of the theologian. Human reason only carries us so far. Ultimately, there has to be the leap in the dark, a new way of knowing: it is called faith.

Jesus is God, a human way of being divine – our bridge between the finite and the infinite. This has some earth-shaking consequences. It means that he mirrors the Father, and indeed the Spirit, for us. He says as much to Philip when that apostle asks him to 'show us the Father': 'Have I been with you all this time, Philip, and you still do not know me? Whoever has seen me has seen the Father' *(John 14:8-9)*. So when we look at the compassionate Christ, we get an inkling as to what the good God is like. It is an image that, historically, Christians have often failed to convey in their catechesis.

Not that all this was clear to the human Jesus from the start. He gradually grew in self awareness and his identity became clearer through the joys and travails of life. Luke tells us that, following Jesus' presentation as an infant in the temple at Jerusalem, Mary and Joseph returned to Galilee, 'And Jesus increased in wisdom, in stature, and in favour with God and men' *(2:22)*. He developed as we humans do. As a human here on earth, was he ever utterly clear about the fact that he was divine? It is a good question.

The gospels are a privileged place for finding Christ. These are accounts of his life and teachings given by Matthew, Mark, Luke, and John. But we

must be clear about what the gospels are. They are certainly historical, but they are not history in the scien-
tific sense. The evangelists set out to give an account
of Jesus' life, yet their main concern was to communicate a religious message. In addition to undeniable
fact, we find parables, canticles, proverbs, and so forth
that are not usually the core stuff of history. However,
the religious message is patently clear. It is a message
of love succinctly expressed by John thus: 'For God so
loved the world that he gave his only Son, so that
everyone who believes in him may not perish but may
have eternal life' *(3:16)*. Imparting a religious message
is the purpose of the gospels, a purpose which they
achieve admirably.

We say that, though the gospels are not history
books, they are indeed historic accounts. One of the
criteria for historic authenticity is the nearness in time
of the historian to the facts he or she is recounting.
Where the gospels are concerned, the authors at least
knew eyewitnesses to the events they describe or may
have been themselves eyewitnesses. The accounts,
after all, were written in about the last third of the first
century. Where history is concerned, this time lapse is
merely the blinking of an eye.

Methodology
The methodology of *In Search of Christ, A Prayer Book
for Seekers* will be on the basis of sessions that will take
key gospel passages which will allow us to delve into
his life and teachings. Individuals may fruitfully use
this book, but it can be even more fruitfully used by
couples, small groups and communities of 'two or
three', even some more. The pattern of the sessions
will be as follows:

1) Opening Prayer

A brief prayer is said, so that the participants may place themselves in the presence of God, followed by a short pause before entering into a gospel sharing. I am aware that some readers may not be believers, so in moments devoted to prayer they may wish to quietly get in touch with themselves and whatever reality gives meaning to their lives.

2) Gospel Sharing or Personal Reflection

Please note there is a brief introduction to the gospel that ought to be read carefully because it should enrich the subsequent sharing or personal reflection. Questions are provided, but participants don't necessarily have to cover them all; it may sometimes be opportune to devote more than one session to a passage. If a question is ever omitted, in general, it should not be No 1. Where couples or groups are concerned, there is a difference between gospel sharing and gospel study. In a gospel study we may appropriately thresh things out and argue about them, even noisily! A gospel sharing tends to be more quiet and prayerful. Some renowned scripture scholars say the best way to deal with the word of God is to ask how the passage under consideration helps or challenges me. What issues does it raise for me? I may then share my insights with other members of a group without trying to force my point of view upon them. We express our thoughts in a spirit of 'this is how this passage challenges me' or 'this is what it says to me ... maybe it helps you ... maybe not'. It is a question of I, me, we, us, rather than you and they. And we don't haggle, clarify maybe. We respect what participants say, believing, as Christians, that the Spirit can speak through anyone; it is not the occasion for putting people right, if we think they are wrong. After all, everyone has ample opportunity to express their own point of view.

Briefly, then, the questions provided on gospel readings are there to help participants reflect on the passage chosen. They go on to calmly and reflectively share their thoughts. A space should be left between contributions, so that folk can think about what has been said. This pays due respect to the contributor.

At the beginning of the sharing (following the perusal of the introductory notes) someone reads the passage aloud, and then there is a pause of three to five minutes as people are left to ponder over it. We should not be afraid of the silences. In the silences the Spirit speaks. The passage may be read a second time (different reader) followed by a further three to five minutes silence. The participants then proceed to make their reflections and avoid being too long-winded.

3) Reality/Action

The word of God is not fully the word of God while in a book or on the lips; it only becomes so when put into practice. The word must be made flesh. The questions are provided to help this process.

4) Spontaneous Prayer

When the group decides upon what precisely they are going to do to put the word of God into practice, they then devote time to spontaneous prayer, or prayer that comes straight from the heart. The author provides examples, but space is left for the prayers and petitions of the participants themselves.

5) The Blessing

The facilitator of the meeting could pronounce the final blessing and, if she wishes, sprinkle the participants with holy water. The session will of course need a facilitator. Yet she or he does not have to do everything; preferably they will also involve others.

6) Hymn
An appropriate hymn may be sung to end the session.
But a hymn is a form of prayer and one may also be
sung among the spontaneous prayers.

Summary of the Method:
1) Opening prayer to place ourselves in God's presence.
2) Gospel sharing (please read no 2 above carefully for
guidance on this key point).
3) Reality/Action (how to put the word of God just
heard into practice).
4) Spontaneous prayer (coming from the heart).
5) Blessing (pronounced by facilitator of the meeting).
6) Hymn (if desired).

   I believe the user will find the method straightforward. The author does share thoughts and prayers
with the reader. The main purpose of these, however,
is to inspire and enrich participation, not to be intru-
sive.

Epoch-making change
An interesting phenomenon since Vatican Council II
is that the Bible is to be found back in the hands of the
laity. It is no longer the sole preserve of the cleric and
the scholar. This is a wholesome development because
it was written by ordinary people for ordinary people
in the first place. Such folk can often be more at home
than intellectuals with the stories, myths, symbols,
songs, poems, dramas, and powerful word pictures
that are the very stuff of which the scriptures are
made. They too are the ones who fish all night and
catch nothing, go out to sow seeds, search diligently
for a badly needed lost coin, or don't have a place to
lay their heads at night.

Not that we wish to downgrade the contribution of scholars in Bible reflection. Far from it. They do the invaluable work of giving us the historic and social settings of the text. But that is not the only purpose of the Bible. Still more important is what the Spirit is inspiring Christians to say about scripture as they relate it to their lives. Ideally, of course, the two contributions should be brought together because they complement each other.

There is still another dimension that to me seems vital. This is personal and intimate. It involves relating my own life experience to the word and to Christ, for we all have our personal, indeed intimate histories. In the case of the present volume, it would mean seeing where Christ entered and made an impact on my own existence. I, for example, have been a missionary most of my life. This often meant leaving persons and places that I held dear and moving on to scenes that were totally new to me. This was often extremely painful. With time, I began to register a most consoling fact. There was one unfailing friend who was always with me. As I left a place he bade me farewell, was with me on the journey and, when I arrived at my destination, was waiting to greet me. Christ was that friend. Again, as I look back down the years, I am amazed at how kind he has been to me, how infinitely patient with me. But we all have our personal stories, and it is important to explore them. Our method makes room for this.

Beginnings

Session 1
The Annunciation

(N.B. The methodology of this volume is straightforward, but I strongly recommend that the introduction be read before the reader begins. It gives the key to the use of the book.)

Opening Prayer

Lord, we place ourselves in your presence. Send us your Spirit to enlighten our minds and open our hearts to your word. We know Jesus is with us because we are gathered in his name, and he tells us '... where two or three are gathered in my name, I am with them.' We also invite our holy mother Mary, the Seat of Wisdom, to be part of our sharing. Amen.

Gospel Sharing (Luke 1:26-38)

In the following passage, Mary is given the momentous news that she will conceive in her womb and bear a son and that he is to be named Jesus. The name, incidentally, means 'Saviour'. He will be great and will be called the Son of the Most High; he will be given the throne of his ancestor David. Mary asks how this can possibly be, since she is a virgin. Gabriel tells her that it will be achieved through the power of the Holy Spirit, and that the one that is to be born of her is to be called the Son of God. Looking back on this event with the gift of hindsight, we are quite aware of what is happening. But understandably Mary is 'much perplexed'. She no doubt realised that Jesus was going to be someone special, possibly even the longed for Messiah, but to grasp that he was to be divine, as the extract suggests, was surely beyond her.

Like any Jew at the time, her awe of El Shaddai, the Most High, would have been absolute. That she should give birth to God's Son could not have entered into her most wild imaginings. These things she would ponder over and struggle with through the years to come. As we reflect on the passage, we have to bear Mary's position in mind. The gospels have not yet been written, nor has there been well-nigh two thousand years analysis of these events by theologians and scripture scholars.

26In the sixth month the angel Gabriel was sent sent by God to a town in Galilee called Nazareth, 27to a virgin engaged to a man whose name was Joseph of the house of David. The virgin's name was Mary. 28And he came to her and said, 'Greetings favoured one! The Lord be with you.' 29But she was much perplexed by his words and pondered what sort of greeting this might be. 30The angel said to her, 'Do not be afraid, Mary, for you have found favour with God. 31And now, you will conceive in your womb and bear a son, and you will name him Jesus. 32He will be great and will be called the Son of the Most High, and the Lord God will give him the throne of his ancestor David. 33He will reign over the house of Jacob forever and of his kingdom there will be no end.' Mary said to the angel, 34'How can this be, since I am a virgin?' 35The angel said to her, 'The Holy Spirit will come upon you, and the power of the Most High will overshadow you; therefore the child to be born will be holy; he will be called the Son of God. 36And now, your relative Elizabeth in her old age has also conceived a son; and this is the sixth month for her who was said to be barren. 37For nothing will be impossible with God.' 38Then Mary said, 'Here am I, the servant of the Lord; let it be with me according to thy word.' Then the angel departed from her.

Questions

1) What do you learn about Jesus from the foregoing passage?

2) What impressed, questioned, or challenged you in the extract?

3) Taking your personal experience of Christ into account, does the passage strike any intimate chords for you? *(Because of the nature of this question, it is provided for personal rather than group reflection.)*

Reality/Action

How do we put the word of God we have heard into practice? Is there something we can do? Or are we doing something that can be done better? Are there attitudes to change? *(The group should decide on some practical outcome.)*

Spontaneous Prayer

1) Merciful Lord, help us to grasp something of the great mystery of how Jesus, the Son of God, took on flesh and blood like ours. And help us to work out, more and more, what this means for our world. Lord hear us.

R. Lord graciously hear us.

2) Lord of wisdom, Mary not only heard the word of God, the Word became flesh in her womb. Give us the grace to put the word of God into practice as she always did. Lord hear us.

R. Lord graciously hear us.

3) God, creator of all, who humbled yourself to become one of us, help us to understand that humility is the foundation of all virtue. Lord hear us.

R. Lord graciously hear us.

The participants may now add their own prayers and petitions.

When these prayers and petitions end, there is the recitation of:
The Lord's Prayer.

Blessing
May we and our world be charged with the power of the Incarnation.
R. Amen,
May we put God's word into practice.
R. Amen.
May we be humble as God is humble.
R. Amen.
And may almighty God bless you, the Father, the Son, and the Holy Spirit.
R. Amen.

Hymn:
An appropriate hymn may be sung.

Session 2
Jesus' identity

Opening Prayer
Lord, we place ourselves in your presence. Send us your Spirit to enlighten our minds and open our hearts to your word. We know Jesus is with us because we are gathered in his name, and he tells us '... where two or three are gathered in my name I am with them.' We also invite our holy mother Mary, the Seat of Wisdom, to be part of our sharing. Amen.

Gospel Sharing (Matthew 1:18-25)
The first chapter of Matthew provides the identity of Jesus. He is the promised Messiah, or Saviour of Israel – 'Jesus' means 'Saviour' – and uniquely conceived of the Holy Spirit. He is, therefore, of God, indeed amazingly he is Emmanuel or 'God with us'. Yet he is also of the royal house of David, because Joseph, of David's lineage, accepts Mary as his wife and Jesus as his son. He is therefore of the human family. He is one of us!

[18]Now the birth of Jesus the Messiah took place in this way. When his mother Mary had been engaged to Joseph, but before they lived together, she was found to be with child from the Holy Spirit. [19]Her husband Joseph, being a righteous man and unwilling to expose her to public disgrace, planned to dismiss her quietly. [20]But just when he resolved to do this, an angel of the Lord appeared to him in a dream and said, 'Joseph, son of David, do not be afraid to take Mary as your wife for the child conceived in her is of the Holy Spirit. [21]She will bear a son, and you are to name him Jesus, for he will save his people from their sins.' [22]All this took place to fulfil what had been spoken by the

Lord through the prophet [Isaiah]: 23'Look, the virgin shall conceive and bear a son, and they shall name him Emmanuel' which means 'God is with us.' 24When Joseph awoke from sleep, he did as the angel of the Lord commanded him: he took her as his wife, 25but had no marital relations with her until she had borne a son: and he named him Jesus.

Questions

1) What do you learn about Jesus from the foregoing passage?

2) What impressed, questioned, or challenged you in the extract?

3) Taking your personal experience of Christ into account, does the passage strike any intimate chords for you? *(Because of the nature of this question, it is provided for personal rather than group reflection.)*

Reality/Action

How do we put the word of God we have heard into practice? Is there something we can do? Or are we doing something that can be done better? Are there attitudes to change? *(The group should decide on some practical outcome.)*

Spontaneous Prayer

1) Gracious God, thank you for Jesus our Saviour, at once true God and true man. Lord hear us.

R. Lord, graciously hear us.

2) Lord, may we learn from the discretion of Mary and sensitivity of Joseph. Lord hear us.

R. Lord graciously hear us.

3) God of wonder, may we never cease to marvel at the words 'Emmanuel ... God is with us.' Lord hear us.

R. Lord graciously hear us.

The participants may now add their own prayers and petitions. When these prayers and petitions end, there is the recitation of:
The Lord's Prayer

Blessing
May we never cease to thank God for the gift of Jesus the Saviour.
R. Amen.
May we treat each other with the delicacy of Mary and Joseph.
R. Amen.
May we always remember 'God is with us.'
R. Amen.
And may almighty God bless you, the Father, the Son, and the Holy Spirit.
R. Amen.

Hymn
An appropriate hymn may be sung.

Session 3
The birth of Jesus

Opening Prayer
Lord, we place ourselves in your presence. Send us your Spirit to enlighten our minds and open our hearts to your word. We know Jesus is with us because we are gathered in his name, and he tells us '... where two or three are gathered in my name, I am with them.' We also invite our holy mother Mary, the Seat of Wisdom, to be part of our sharing. Amen.

Gospel Sharing (Luke 2:1-14)
Luke gives us the story of Jesus' birth, a story which came from the first eyewitnesses to his life, including, most probably, Mary (cf Luke 1:2). It is an event of world importance: important for Israel, important for Rome. Hence it is set in the context of the census decreed by Augustus. In Luke the shepherds are called to be witnesses to this cosmic happening, in Matthew it is the Magi. These witnesses then disappear off the scene, so that when Jesus appears in the wilderness to be baptised by John, his identity is not generally known. It is noteworthy that the first ones to whom the newborn babe is revealed are the little ones of the earth, humble shepherds. The last are first (cf Mark 10:31). It is also noteworthy that Jesus was numbered among the homeless on the first night he spent on earth. In God's design, he is identified with all those who do not have a place to lay their heads (cf Luke 9:58).
¹In those days a decree went out from the Emperor Augustus that all the world would be registered. ²This was the first registration and was taken when Quirinius was governor of Syria. ³All went to their own towns to be registered. ⁴Joseph also went from

the town of Nazareth in Galilee to Judea, to the city of David called Bethlehem, because he was descended from the house and family of David. [5]He went to be registered with Mary, to whom he was engaged and who was expecting a child. [6]While they were there, the time came for her to deliver her child. [7]And she gave birth to her firstborn son and wrapped him in bands of cloth, and laid him in a manger, because there was no place for him in the inn.

[8]In that region there were shepherds living in the fields, keeping watch over their flocks by night. [9]Then an angel of the Lord stood before them, and the glory of the Lord shone around them, and they were terrified. [10]But the angel said to them, 'Do not be afraid; for see – I am bringing you good news of great joy for all the people: [11]to you is born this day in the city of David a Saviour, who is the Messiah, the Lord. [12]This will be a sign for you: you will find a child wrapped in bands of cloth and lying in a manger.' [13]And suddenly there was with the angel a multitude of the heavenly host, praising God and saying,

[14]'Glory to God in the highest heaven,
and on earth peace among those
who are God's friends!'

Questions

1) What do you learn about Jesus from the foregoing passage?

2) What impressed, questioned, or challenged you in the extract?

3) Taking your personal experience of Christ into account, does the passage strike any intimate chords for you? *(Because of the nature of this question, it is provided for personal rather than group reflection.)*

Reality/Action
How do we put the word of God we have heard into practice? Is there something we can do? Or are we doing something that can be done better? Are there attitudes to change? *(The group should decide on some practical outcome.)*

Spontaneous Prayer
1) Loving God, there is beauty and poetry surrounding Jesus' birth. This is only right because his coming surely is good news. Yet there was hardship too for the Holy Family. Grant, Lord, that while we admire the beauty, we strive to understand the suffering. By his cross, Jesus would eventually redeem the world. Lord hear us.
R. Lord, graciously hear us.
2) Lord of heaven and earth, with the host of angels we sing, 'Glory to God in the highest heaven, and on earth peace among those who are God's friends!' Lord hear us.
R. Lord graciously hear us.
3) Lord, we thank you as Jesus takes his place alongside the little ones of the earth. May we always do likewise. Lord hear us.
R. Lord graciously hear us.
The participants may add their own prayers and petitions. When these prayers and petitions end, there is the recitation of:
The Lord's Prayer.

Blessing
May we ever love poetry and beauty.
R. Amen.
May we value suffering.
R. Amen.

May we stand by the little ones of our world.
R. Amen.
And may almighty God bless you, the Father, the Son,
and the Holy Spirit.
R. Amen.

Hymn
An appropriate hymn may be sung.

Session 4
Word made flesh

Opening Prayer

Lord, we place ourselves in your presence. Send us your Spirit to enlighten our minds and open our hearts to your word. We know Jesus is with us because we are gathered in his name, and he tells us '... where two or three are gathered in my name, I am with them.' We also invite our holy mother Mary, the Seat of Wisdom, to be part of our sharing. Amen.

Gospel Sharing (John 1:1-5, 9-14)

The following passage is a Prologue to John's gospel. In it John gives us his view of Christ, so the extract is important in terms of knowing Jesus. We need to look at the expression 'the Word'. Who is the Word? The human Jesus was born on to this earth in time, about 2000 years ago. Yet, being divine and Second Person of the Blessed Trinity, he of course existed from all eternity as 'the Word'. John regards Christ as a divine being, God's Word, who is also light and life and God's only Son; he comes into the world and becomes flesh. Many did not accept him, but he empowered those who did to become the children of God and share in God's fullness. In the scriptures, the term 'world' is used in two senses. Firstly it refers to God's marvellous creation yet also on occasions to the world of sin. We have to judge the meaning from the context. In John 'glory' often translates as 'love'.

[1]In the beginning was the Word, and the Word was with God. [2]He was in the beginning with God. [3]All things came into being through him, and without him not one thing came. What has come into being [4]in him was life, and the life was the light of all people.

5The light shines in the darkness, and the darkness did not overcome it ... 9The true light, which enlightens everyone, was coming into the world.

10He was in the world, and the world came into being through him; yet the world did not know him. 11He came to what was his own, and his own people did not accept him. 12But to all who received him, who believed in his name, he gave power to become children of God, 13who were born not of blood or the will of the flesh or the will of humans, but of God.

14And the Word became flesh and lived among us, and we have seen his glory as of a father's only son, full of grace and truth.

Questions
1) What do you learn about Jesus from the foregoing passage?
2) What impressed, questioned, or challenged you in the extract?
3) Taking your personal experience of Christ into account, does the passage strike any intimate chords for you? *(Because of the nature of this question, it is provided for personal rather than group reflection.)*

Reality/Action
How do we put the word of God we have heard into practice? Is there something we can do? Or are we doing something that can be done better? Are there attitudes to change? *(The group should decide on some practical outcome.)*

Spontaneous Prayer
1) Gracious God, we thank you that the Word became flesh. May the wonder of this never leave us. Lord hear us.
R. Lord graciously hear us.
2) Lord, we eagerly receive you in our midst, so, as you promised, give us the power to be children of God and share in God's fullness. Lord hear us.
R. Lord graciously hear us.
3) Father, may your only begotten Son Jesus, full of grace and truth, be ever honoured and glorified. Lord hear us.
R. Lord graciously hear us.
The participants may now add their own prayers and petitions. When these prayers and petitions end, there is the recitation of:
The Lord's Prayer

Blessing
May God's word become flesh in our lives.
R. Amen.
May we receive God's fullness.
R. Amen.
May Christ be our light and life.
R. Amen.
And may almighty God bless you, the Father, the Son, and the Holy Spirit.
R. Amen.

Hymn
An appropriate hymn may be sung.

Session 5
Epiphany: Magi visit Jesus

Opening Prayer
Lord, we place ourselves in your presence. Send us your Spirit to enlighten our minds and open our hearts to your word. We know Jesus is with us because we are gathered in his name, and he tells us '... where two or three are gathered in my name, I am with them.' We also invite our holy mother Mary, the Seat of Wisdom, to be part of our sharing. Amen.

Gospel Sharing (Matthew 2:1-12)
The Magi, wise men from the East, come to visit Jesus directed by a star. The significant point is that they are not Jewish, not of the chosen people. They are in fact gentiles and do not have the scriptures to guide them. The sad reality is that those who have the scriptures do not believe. Interestingly, the Magi use the title 'king of the Jews' in referring to Jesus; it is used once more when Jesus is crucified. Again it is gentiles who recognise the truth about him (Matthew 25:54). God frustrates the plans of Herod by Jesus' return from Egypt, and the designs of those who crucify him, by his resurrection from the dead. Once more, surrounding the birth of Jesus, there is beauty:
Now is the night of the Child and the Star,
The night of the long dreams that suddenly are ...
(Chris Macgill)
But there is also trouble and suffering. It is inevitably part of the life of Christ as it is of all humans. Jesus tells us that we must be ready to take up our cross daily and follow him. However, he does assure us that, with his help, the yoke is easy and the burden light. And there is always the beauty. The prophecy mentioned in the passage

is that of Micah (5:2). Matthew worked with a mixed community of Jews and gentiles and, out of respect for the Jewish presence, is keen to point out connections with the Old Testament.

[1]In the time of King Herod, after Jesus was born in Bethlehem in Judea, wise men from the East came to Jerusalem, [2]asking, 'Where is the child that has been born king of the Jews? Because we observed his star at its rising and have come to pay him homage.' [3]When King Herod heard this, he was frightened, and all Jerusalem with him; [4]and calling together all the chief priests and scribes of the people, he inquired of them where the Messiah was to be born. [5]They told him, 'In Bethlehem of Judea; for so it has been written by the prophet: [6]"And you Bethlehem in the land of Judah, are by no means least among the rulers of Judah; for from you shall come a ruler who is to shepherd my people Israel."'

[7]Then Herod secretly called for the wise men and learned from them the exact time when the star appeared. [8]Then he sent them to Bethlehem, saying, 'Go and search diligently for the child; and when you have found him, bring me word so that I may also go and pay him homage.' [9]When they had heard the king, they set out; and there, ahead of them, went the star that they had seen at its rising until it stopped over the place where the child was. [10]When they saw that the star had stopped, they were overwhelmed with joy. [11]On entering the house, they saw the child with Mary his mother; and they knelt down and paid him homage. Then, opening their treasure chests, they offered him gifts of gold, frankincense, and myrrh. [12]And having been warned in a dream not to return to Herod, they left for their own country by another road.

Questions
1) What do you learn about Jesus from the foregoing passage?
2) What impressed, questioned, or challenged you in the extract?
3) Taking your personal experience of Christ into account, does the passage strike any intimate chords for you? *(Because of the nature of this question, it is provided for personal rather than group reflection.)*

Reality/Action
How do we put the word of God we have heard into practice? Is there something we can do? Or are we doing something that can be done better? Are there attitudes to change? *(The group should decide on some practical outcome.)*

Spontaneous Prayer
(I depart somewhat from our usual pattern to use the evocative poem of Chris Macgill, daughter, incidentally, of Patrick Macgill the renowned Donegal poet and novelist. It reads like a modern psalm.)
Now is the night of the Child and the Star,
The night of the long dreams that suddenly are,
The night of the angels, the night of the awe,
The night of the stable and cradling straw.

Now is the night of the song and the wings,
The night of the shepherds, the night of the kings,
The night of the long dreams that suddenly are,
Now is the night of the Child and the Star.

The participants may now add their own prayers and petitions. When these prayers and petitions end, there is the recitation of:
The Lord's Prayer.

Blessing
May we rejoice in the night of the Child and the Star.
R. Amen.
May we be filled with wonder in the night of the song
and the night of the wings.
R. Amen.
May we thrill at the long dreams that suddenly are.
R. Amen.
And may almighty God bless you, the Father, the Son,
and the Holy Spirit.
R. Amen.

Hymn
An appropriate hymn may be sung.

Session 6
Jesus the refugee

Opening Prayer
Lord, we place ourselves in your presence. Send us your
Spirit to enlighten our minds and open our hearts to
your word. We know that Jesus is with us because we
are gathered in his name, and he tells us '... where two
or three are gathered in my name, I am with them.'
We also invite our holy mother Mary, the Seat of
Wisdom, to be with us in our sharing. Amen.

Gospel Sharing (Matthew 2:13-15; 19-23)
*When the Magi left, the Lord warned Joseph in a dream
to flee to Egypt with Jesus and Mary, because Herod
wanted to kill the child. He feared that the baby 'who has
been born king of the Jews' would deprive his own children of the throne. So the Holy Family quickly became
refugees, having already endured homelessness. Jesus is
indeed being identified with the hapless ones of the earth.
They remained in Egypt until the death of Herod, thereby
fulfilling the prophecy of Hosea (11:1). On returning,
Joseph went to the land of Israel, but when he heard that
Archelaus was king, he went to Nazareth in Galilee.
Once more, through the designs of God, Jesus is to stand
by the despised ones. Galilee was looked down upon by
the Jews and given the disparaging title 'Galilee of the
gentiles'. Joseph reminds us of another son of Israel, or
Jacob, also called Joseph and also a dreamer (made famil-
iar to many modern young people through Andrew Lloyd
Webber's musical entitled, 'Joseph and the Amazing
Technicolour Dreamcoat'). And there is a parallel with
Moses too. According to Jewish legends, Wise Men gave
information to Pharaoh regarding Moses, just as Wise*

Men gave information to Herod regarding Jesus. Matthew worked with a mixed community of Jews and gentiles. Hence, out of deference to his own people, Old Testament connections were important. The final words of the passage, 'He will be a Nazarene' are from Isaiah.

[13]Now after they [the Magi] had left, an angel of the Lord appeared to Joseph in a dream and said, 'Get up, take the child and his mother and flee to Egypt, and remain there until I tell you; for Herod is about to search for the child, to destroy him.' [14]Then Joseph got up, took the child and his mother by night, and went to Egypt, [15]and remained there until the death of Herod. This was to fulfil what had been spoken by the Lord through the prophet, 'out of Egypt I have called my son ...'

[19]When Herod died, an angel of the Lord suddenly appeared in a dream to Joseph in Egypt and said, [20]'Get up, take the child and his mother, and go to the land of Israel, for those who were seeking the child's life are dead.' [21]Then Joseph got up, took the child and his mother, and went to the land of Israel. [22]But when he heard that Archelaus was ruling over Judea in place of his father, Herod, he was afraid to go there. And after being warned in a dream, he went to the district of Galilee. [23]There he made his home in a town called Nazareth, so that what had been spoken through the prophets might be fulfilled, 'He will be called a Nazarene.'

Questions

1) What do you learn about Jesus from the foregoing passage?

2) What impressed, questioned, or challenged you in the extract?

3) Taking your personal experience of Christ into

account, does the passage strike any intimate chords for you? *(Because of the nature of this question, it is provided for personal rather than group reflection.)*

Reality/Action

How do we put the word of God we have heard into practice? Is there something we can do? Or are we doing something that can be done better? Are there attitudes to change? *(The group should decide on some practical outcome.)*

Spontaneous Prayer

1) God of justice and peace, how quickly is your Son threatened by violence. Help all people to reject brutality and follow the paths of active non-violence, dialogue, and reason. Lord hear us.

R. Lord, graciously hear us.

2) God of compassion, grant that we be welcoming to the refugee and the stranger, mindful that Jesus, Mary, and Joseph were themselves hapless refugees in the land of Egypt. Lord hear us.

R. Lord, graciously hear us.

3) God of courage, may we stand steadfastly by the despised of the earth, as Jesus did. Lord hear us.

R. Lord, graciously hear us.

The participants may now add their own prayers and petitions. When these prayers and petitions end, there is the recitation of:

The Lord's Prayer

Blessing
May we persevere in paths of justice and peace.
R. Amen
May we welcome the stranger.
R. Amen.
May we identify with the despised.
R. Amen.
And may almighty God bless you, the Father, the Son,
and the Holy Spirit.
R. Amen.

Hymn
An appropriate hymn may be sung.

Session 7
Lost Child!

Opening Prayer
Lord, we place ourselves in your presence. Send us your
Spirit to enlighten our minds and open our hearts to
your word. We know that Jesus is with us because we
are gathered in his name, and he tells us '... where two
or three are gathered in my name, I am with them.'
We also invite our holy mother Mary, the Seat of
Wisdom, to be with us in our sharing. Amen.

Gospel Sharing (Luke 2:41-52)
In the annunciation an angel proclaims that Jesus is
God's Son (Luke 1:35); in the following passage Jesus at
the age of twelve makes the clear statement that God is his
Father; at his baptism in the Jordan, age thirty, God's
own voice from heaven proclaims, 'You are my beloved
Son' (3:22-23). So at Christ's birth, as a boy of twelve,
and as an adult the same claim is made; it is a satisfac-
tory sequence. Luke intended it to be such. Yet the people
of Nazareth were later unaware of his identity (Luke
4:16-30), because he went back with Mary and Joseph to
Nazareth after the episode related here and was obedient
to them, probably by not provoking any more revealing
incidents. To what extent did Jesus himself understand
the statement implying that God was his Father? Only to
some extent. Elsewhere Luke informs us that this was very
much a learning phase in the life of Christ (2:22).
Undoubtedly he was a highly intelligent child and filled
the teachers in the temple with admiration. However, to
imagine that there was a great outpouring of divine wis-
dom would be a misconception. Here was a precocious
and curious child full of 'whys', who could also give a

telling answer. He had been attentive at his synagogue in Nazareth and was filled with the Holy Spirit. This boyhood incident is proper to Luke's gospel and must have come to him from a source independent from the other evangelists.

41Now every year his parents went to Jerusalem for the festival of the Passover. 42And when he was twelve years old, they went up as usual for the festival. 43When the festival was ended and they started to return, the boy Jesus stayed behind in Jerusalem, but his parents did not know it. 44Assuming that he was in the group of travellers, they went a day's journey. Then they started to look for him among their relatives and friends. 45When they did not find him, they returned to Jerusalem to search for him. 46After three days they found him in the temple, sitting among the teachers, listening to them and asking them questions. 47And all who heard him were amazed at his understanding and his answers. 48When his parents saw him they were astonished; and his mother said to him, 'Child, why have you treated us like this? Look, your father and I have been searching for you in great anxiety.' 49He said to them, 'Why were you searching for me? Did you not know that I must be in my Father's house?' 50But they did not understand what he said to them. 51Then he went down with them and came to Nazareth, and was obedient to them. His mother treasured all these things in her heart.

52And Jesus increased in wisdom and in years, and in divine and human favour.

Questions

1) What did you learn about Jesus from the foregoing passage?

2) What impressed, questioned, or challenged you in the extract?

3) Taking your personal experience of Christ into account, does the passage strike any intimate chords for you? *(Because of the nature of this question, it is provided for personal rather than group reflection.)*

Reality/Action

How do we put the word of God we have heard into practice? Is there something we can do? Or are we doing something that can be done better? Are there attitudes to change? *(The group should decide on some practical outcome.)*

Spontaneous Prayer

1) God of wisdom, like the teachers in the temple we wonder at the boy Jesus. May we avail of this opportunity to get to know and love him a little better. Lord hear us.

R. Lord graciously hear us.

2) Merciful Lord, like Mary and Joseph, many parents lose children. Some die prematurely, through sickness or violence. Some disappear never to be found again. How immense, Lord, is the suffering of those parents. Often, not even time, that great healer, is capable of salving the wounds. Overwhelm their sufferings, Lord, with the comfort of your infinite love, and fill their hearts with the expectation of being reunited with their loved ones in your kingdom. Lord hear us.

R. Lord graciously hear us.

3) Lord, help us to ponder in our hearts the words and actions of Jesus as intensely as his mother Mary did.

Lord hear us.
R. Lord graciously hear us.
The participants may now add their own prayers and petitions. When these prayers and petitions end, there is the recitation of:
The Lord's Prayer

Blessing
May the Son of God be praised.
R. Amen.
May the Lord comfort distraught parents.
R. Amen.
May we ever ponder the words and deeds of Jesus.
R. Amen.
And may almighty God bless you, the Father, the Son, and the Holy Spirit.
R. Amen.

Hymn
An appropriate hymn may be sung.

In the Midst of Things
(In medias res)

Session 8
Baptism of Jesus

Opening Prayer
Lord, we place ourselves in your presence. Send us your Spirit to enlighten our minds and open our hearts to your word. We know Jesus is with us because we are gathered in his name, and he tells us '... where two or three are gathered in my name, I am with them.' We also invite our holy mother Mary, the Seat of Wisdom, to be part of our sharing. Amen.

Gospel Sharing (Matthew 3:13-17)
When Jesus comes to be baptised in the Jordan, John the Baptist recognises the anomaly: it is Jesus, not he, who should be doing the baptising. Jesus, however, accepts baptism from John as part of God's plan to save humankind and build a kingdom of love. One is touched by the meekness and humility of Christ. John too has a healthy sense of his own abjection. These are not vainglorious men. John's baptism is, of course, 'a baptism of repentance for the forgiveness of sins'; it is not our present Christian sacrament. John has baptised with water, but Jesus will do so with the Holy Spirit. The baptism is a Trinitarian event: Jesus is being baptised, the Spirit descends, and the voice of the Father is heard in the heavens. God is three. The mystery is there implicitly in the Old Testament; in the New, Christ makes it explicit. Very recently on television I heard a man say that he rejected Christianity, because the mystery of the Trinity is based on a mathematical absurdity, namely, that 3=1. This is

to misunderstand us. We are not saying that one person equals three persons, but that there are three divine persons and one divine nature. Three of one and one of another. This is not against reason, no more than it is against reason to say that three feet equals one yard. What do we mean by 'nature' and what by 'person'? These philosophical realities cannot simply be put under a microscope. The problem is that in our human experience we always encounter one person and one nature. If Jesus hadn't revealed the mystery of the Trinity, we could never have arrived at it using our own reason. Note that the gospel does not say that the Spirit of God was a dove descending, but 'like' a dove. Our human words always fall short when we come to talk of the things of God. Yet, as a recent popular song put it, 'words are all we have'. The voice of the Father declares that Jesus is his Son, the Beloved. His tenderness is not just for a being who is divine; it is also for the human Jesus.

¹³Then Jesus came from Galilee to John at the Jordan, to be baptised by him. ¹⁴John would have prevented him, saying, 'I need to be baptised by you, and do you come to me?' ¹⁵But Jesus answered him, 'Let it be so now; for it is proper for us in this way to fulfil all righteousness.' Then he consented. ¹⁶And when Jesus had been baptised, just as he came up from the water, suddenly the heavens were opened to him and he saw the Spirit of God descending like a dove and alighting on him. ¹⁷And a voice from heaven said, 'This is my Son, the Beloved, with whom I am well pleased.'

Questions

1) What do you learn about Jesus from the foregoing passage?

2) What impressed, questioned, or challenged you in the extract?

3) Taking your personal experience of Christ into account, does the passage strike any intimate chords for you? *(Because of the nature of this question, it is provided for personal rather than group reflections.)*

Reality/Action
How do we put the word of God we have heard into practice? Is there something we can do? Or are we doing something that can be done better? Are there attitudes to change? *(The group should decide on some practical outcome.)*

Spontaneous Prayer
1) Lord our God, who did not despise to become one of us, grant that we may share something of the humility of Jesus and John the Baptist. Lord hear us.
R. Lord graciously hear us.
2) Merciful Lord, may we never cease to be grateful for the greatest day of our lives: the day when we were baptised with water and the Holy Spirit, became members of the body of Christ (the Christian community), and heirs to the kingdom of heaven. Lord hear us.
R. Lord graciously hear us.
3) Almighty God, three in one, may the Father, Son, and Holy Spirit be forever honoured and glorified. Lord hear us.
R. Lord graciously hear us.
The participants may add their own prayers and petitions. When these prayers and petitions end, there is the recitation of:
The Lord's Prayer

Blessing
May we, like Jesus, be meek and humble of heart.
R. Amen.
May we live our baptism.
R. Amen,
May God the Father, Son, and Holy Spirit be praised forever.
R. Amen.
And may almighty God bless you, the Father, the Son, and the Holy Spirit.
R. Amen.

Hymn
An appropriate hymn may be sung.

Session 9
Jesus tempted

Opening Prayer

Lord, we place ourselves in your presence. Send us your Spirit to enlighten our minds and open our hearts to your word. We know Jesus is with us because we are gathered in his name and he tells us '... where two or three are gathered in my name, I am with them.' We also invite our holy mother Mary, the Seat of Wisdom, to be part of our sharing. Amen.

Gospel Sharing (Matthew 4:1-11)

Jesus is led into the wilderness by the Spirit who is active throughout the whole history of salvation, from the moment of hovering over the waters at the dawn of creation right up to the present day. In tempting Jesus, the devil tries to turn God's kingdom into a worldly one. He wants Jesus to change stones into bread, but he will do this only for others, not for himself. He is offered all the kingdoms of the earth. He is indeed given all power in heaven and on earth by God, yet he does not seek it for himself. Some of the language used in these temptations was used when the Jews were tempted to rebel in the desert on their forty years journey to the Promised Land (cf. Deuteronomy chapters 6-8). Again Matthew, who worked with a mixed community of Jews and gentiles, liked to make connections with the Old Testament for the Jews among them. Having shown Satan that he is Son of God and serves God alone, Jesus summarily dismisses him. One of the most moving things about this episode is the realisation that Jesus endured temptation just as we do ourselves. He is totally human. However, he staunchly resisted the tempter, even the extreme seduction of power and possessions that can prove the undoing of even good people.

[1]Then Jesus was led by the Spirit into the wilderness to be tempted by the devil. [2]He fasted for forty days and forty nights, and afterwards he was famished. [3]The tempter came and said to him, 'If you are the Son of God, command these stones to become loaves of bread.' [4]But he answered, 'It is written, "One does not live by bread alone, but by every word that comes from the mouth of God."'

[5]Then the devil took him to the holy city and placed him on the pinnacle of the temple, [6]saying to him, 'If you are the Son of God, throw yourself down; for it is written: "He will command his angels concerning you." and "On their hands they will bear you up, so that you will not dash your foot against a stone."' [7]Jesus said to him, 'Again it is written, "Do not put the Lord your God to the test."'

[8]Again the devil took him to a very high mountain and showed him all the kingdoms of the world and their splendour, [9]and he said to him, 'All these I will give you, if you will fall down and worship me.' [10]Jesus said to him, 'Away with you Satan! for it is written, "Worship the Lord your God and serve only God." '

[11]The devil left him, and suddenly angels came and waited on him.

Questions
1) What do you learn about Jesus from the foregoing passage?
2) What impressed, questioned, or challenged you in the extract?
3) Taking your personal experience of Christ into account, does the passage strike any intimate chords for you? *(Because of the nature of this question, it is provided for personal rather than group reflection.)*

Reality/Action

How do we put the word of God we have heard into practice? Is there something we can do? Or are we doing something that can be done better? Are there attitudes to change? *(The group should decide on some practical outcome.)*

Spontaneous Prayer

1) Lord God, thank you for the gift of your Son Jesus, who shares our human lot, even to the extent of undergoing temptation. May we learn from his steadfastness. Lord hear us.

R. Lord graciously hear us.

2) All powerful God, without you we can do nothing. Be our strength in times of temptation. Lord hear us.

R. Lord graciously hear us.

3) Good and gracious God, save us from the false lure of worldly power and possessions. Lord hear us.

R. Lord graciously hear us.

The participants may now add their own prayers and petitions. When these prayers and petitions end, there is the recitation of:

The Lord's Prayer

Blessing

May we, like Christ, summarily dismiss Satan.

R. Amen.

May we reject the fool's gold of his promises.

R. Amen.

And may almighty God bless you, the Father, the Son, and the Holy Spirit.

R. Amen.

Hymn

An appropriate hymn may be sung.

Session 10
Wedding feast of Cana

Opening Prayer

Lord, we place ourselves in your presence. Send us your Spirit to enlighten our minds and open our hearts to your word. We know that Jesus is with us because we are gathered in his name, and he tells us '... where two or three are gathered in my name, I am with them.' We also invite our holy mother Mary, the Seat of Wisdom, to be part of our sharing. Amen.

Gospel Sharing (John 2:1-11)

This is a touching story. Since the young couple ran out of wine, probably they were not rich. As on many other occasions in the gospel, Jesus identifies and sympathises with the happenings in the lives of ordinary people and works a miracle – his first in fact – to solve their problem. Mary plays an important role in this event. She informs Jesus of the plight of the newly married pair. Jesus is thrown somewhat by her implicit request, because his understanding is that his time for responding to such a petition has not yet come. Humanly speaking, he was put in a quandary, which shows him struggling with his identity and destiny. To see him as an assured know-all would be a mistake. Obviously, he was challenged to turn to the Spirit and discern. At first, he seems to respond to Mary in an offhand fashion, addressing her as 'woman'. But in their culture this was a solemn and respectful form of address. It was for God alone to decide when Jesus would disclose himself; a request from his mother would not be enough. No doubt Mary was hopeful that God would take pity on these young folk, because she said to the waiters, 'Do whatever he tells you.' Indeed her hope was fulfilled, for Jesus performed his first miracle. Jesus' miracles were not worked with a view to astounding people, rather was it with the end of giving glory to God, who was present in him, and to strengthen the faith of the disciples. So glory was given to God, Mary's hope was fulfilled, and the wine supply was marvellously replenished, as is borne out by the statement of the head waiter, or steward. The first words of the passage, 'On the third day' mean that it was three days after the call of Nathaniel, recorded in the previous chapter. The water was kept in the jars, not for purposes of hygiene, but for Jewish purification rites.

[1]On the third day there was a wedding in Cana of Galilee, and the mother of Jesus was there. [2]Jesus and his disciples had also been invited to the wedding. [3]When the wine gave out, the mother of Jesus said to him, 'They have no wine.' [4]And Jesus said to her, 'Woman, what concern is that to you and to me? My hour is not yet come.' [5]His mother said to the servants, 'Do whatever he tells you.' [6]Now standing there were six stone water jars for the Jewish rites of purification, each holding twenty or thirty gallons. [7]Jesus said to them, 'Fill the jars with water.' And they filled them to the brim. [8]He said to them, 'Now draw out some and take it to the chief steward.' So they took it. [9]When the chief steward had tasted the water that had become wine, and did not know where it came from (though the servants who had drawn the water knew), the steward called the bridegroom [10]and said to him, 'Everyone serves the good wine first, and then the inferior wine after the guests have become drunk. But you have kept the good wine until now.' [11]Jesus did this, the first of his signs, in Cana of Galilee, and revealed his glory; and his disciples believed in him.

Questions

1) What do you learn about Jesus from the foregoing passage?

2) What impressed, questioned, or challenged you in the extract?

3) Taking your personal experience of Christ into account, does the passage strike any intimate chords for you? *(Because of the nature of this question, it is provided for personal rather than group reflection.)*

Reality/Action

How do we put the word of God we have heard into practice? Is there something we can do? Or are we doing something that can be done better? Are there attitudes to change? *(The group should decide on some practical outcome.)*

Spontaneous Prayer

1) Lord, we thank you wholeheartedly for your Son Jesus. Such is his compassion that he is often referred to simply as 'Jesus the Compassion of God'. Lord hear us.
R. Lord graciously hear us.

2) God of kindness, may we be in touch with and, if necessary, moved by the plight of ordinary people as were Jesus and Mary, who, like most of us, were themselves ordinary folk. Lord hear us.

R. Lord graciously hear us.

3) Almighty God, we glorify you for manifesting your power through Jesus. May the witness of his miracles increase our poor faith. Lord hear us.

R. Lord graciously hear us.

The participants may now add their own prayers and petitions. When these prayers and petitions end, there is the recitation of:

The Lord's Prayer

Blessing
May we be compassionate as Jesus was compassionate.
R. Amen.
May we be sensitively aware of others as Mary was.
R. Amen.
May we ever give glory to God.
R. Amen.
And may almighty God bless you, the Father, the Son,
and the Holy Spirit.
R. Amen

Hymn
An appropriate hymn may be sung.

Session 11
Jesus launches his mission in Galilee

Opening Prayer
Lord, we place ourselves in your presence. Send us your Spirit to enlighten our minds and open our hearts to your word. We know Jesus is with us because we are gathered in his name, and he tells us '... where two or three are gathered in my name, I am with them.' We also invite our holy mother Mary, the Seat of Wisdom, to be part of our sharing. Amen.

Gospel Sharing (Mark 1:1, 14)
Says Bishop Peter Price, 'The text that throws open to me the challenge of our times is Mark 1:1: "This is the gospel of Jesus Christ the Son of God".' He goes on to explain that 'gospel' is a term used to describe Roman propaganda of victories in battle on the borders of the empire: Mark steals the term and uses it to a new advantage. In describing Jesus as 'Son of God,' Mark is also jousting at the titles offered to the Roman emperor on the coins: 'Caesar – Divine son of God,' and points to the authentic 'Anointed One' – Christ Jesus, 'who saves his people'. The text presents Jesus as the one who offers a gospel – good news of victories over the powers and principalities which have governed and controlled human affairs; offering a kingdom of justice love and peace. Following on what Price says, it is obvious that the moment when Jesus launches his mission in Galilee with the clarion call: 'The time is fulfilled, and the kingdom of God has come near; repent and believe in the good news' is one of the great moments of history. Through sin we humans had totally wrong-footed ourselves, done something that of ourselves we could not put right. The offence was to God and only

someone who was both human and divine could repair the damage. The ingenious answer came in Jesus the Saviour. The word gospel comes from the Anglo-Saxon 'god spel' which means the good story. When Jesus calls for us to repent, he is not calling for our conventional forms of penance, such as fasting or sleepless, all-night vigils. The Greek word used in the early texts is 'metanoia', which is much more radical. It urges a complete change of heart, not just a donning of sackcloth and pouring on of ashes. That is not to depreciate conventional forms of penance such as fasting, merely to point out what the gospel says.

[1]The beginning of the good news of Jesus Christ, the Son of God ...[14]Now after John was arrested, Jesus came to Galilee, proclaiming the good news of God, and saying, 'The time is fulfilled, and the kingdom of God has come near; repent and believe in the good news.'

Questions

1) What do you learn about Christ from the foregoing passage?

2) What impressed, questioned, or challenged you in the extract?

3) Taking your personal experience of Christ into account, does the passage strike any intimate chords for you? *(Because of the nature of this question, it is provided for personal rather than group reflection.)*

Reality/Action

How do we put the word of God we have heard into practice? Is there something we can do? Or are we doing something that can be done better? Are there attitudes to change? *(The group should decide on some practical outcome.)*

Spontaneous Prayers
1) God of the good news, may we always be open to
your glad tidings and, like Mary, ponder them in our
hearts. Then may your word become flesh in our lives.
Lord hear us.
R. Lord graciously hear us.
2) Lord of openness, help us to widely cast the seeds
of your good news among our brothers and sisters.
Lord hear us.
R. Lord graciously hear us.
3) Redeeming God, how can we ever thank you suffi-
ciently for such a wonderful Saviour? Help us to do so
to the ultimate extent of our poor human capabilities.
Lord hear us.
R. Lord graciously hear us.
*The participants may now add their own prayers and
petitions. When the prayers and petitions end, there is the
recitation of:*
The Lord's Prayer

Blessing
May we ever rejoice in the good news.
R. Amen.
May we ponder it in our hearts.
R. Amen.
May we put it into practice in our lives.
R. Amen.
And may almighty God bless you, the Father, the Son,
and the Holy Spirit.
R. Amen.

Hymn
An appropriate hymn may be sung.

Session 12
The Beatitudes

Opening Prayer
Lord, we place ourselves in your presence. Send us your Spirit to enlighten our minds and open our hearts to your word. We know Jesus is with us because we are gathered in his name, and he tells us '... where two or three are gathered in my name, I am with them.' We also invite our holy mother Mary, the Seat of Wisdom, to be part of our sharing. Amen.

Gospel Sharing (Matthew 5:3-10)
In the following passage we have the Eight Beatitudes. A 'beatitude' is a declaration of blessedness, because of virtue or good fortune. The Beatitudes are part of Jesus' Sermon on the Mount and remind us of how Moses received the Ten Commandments on Mount Sinai. Along with the Ten Commandments the Eight Beatitudes stand as testimony of what God wants from us. They are a graphic statement of the teaching and core values of Jesus. As such we can learn much about the person of Christ from them. Whereas the phrase 'Thou shalt not' occurs frequently in the Ten Commandments, the Beatitudes use the positive 'Blessed are ...' Since not all the people in Matthew's community were poor, he adds the spiritualising phrase 'poor in spirit'. Luke says simply 'you who are poor' and this is probably what Christ said originally. Better off people can also be blessed if they make their own Christ's option with the poor (cf Luke 4:16-21), identify with them, love them, share with them, and simplify their own lifestyle. The Beatitudes propose high ideals. However, the Lord is most certainly with us in our efforts to live them; we are not left on our own. The paradox is that the high ideals

which the Beatitudes present are, in fact, the most practical way to live our lives. Life will show us this. And the promises accompanying the Beatitudes are stupendous.

³'Blessed are the poor in spirit, for theirs is the kingdom of heaven.

⁴'Blessed are they who mourn, for they will be comforted.

⁵'Blessed are the meek, for they will inherit the earth.
⁶'Blessed are those who hunger and thirst for justice, for they will be filled.

⁷'Blessed are the merciful, for they will receive mercy.
⁸'Blessed are the pure in heart, for they will see God.
⁹'Blessed are the peacemakers, for they will be called children of God.

¹⁰'Blessed are those who are persecuted for righteousness' sake, for theirs is the kingdom of heaven.'

Questions
1) What do you learn about Jesus from the foregoing passage?
2) What impressed, questioned, or challenged you in the extract?
3) Taking your personal experience of Christ into account, does the passage strike any intimate chords for you? *(Because of the nature of this question, it is provided for personal rather than group reflection.)*

Reality/Action
How do we put the word of God we have heard into practice? Is there something we can do? Or are we doing something that can be done better? Are there attitudes to change? *(The group should decide on some practical outcome.)*

Spontaneous Prayer

1) God of wisdom, teach us that the most practical way to live our lives is, with your help, to observe the Beatitudes proposed by Jesus. Lord hear us.

R. Lord graciously hear us.

2) God of simple things, if we are not poor, help us to simplify our lives and freely make an option with the poor. Lord hear us.

R. Lord graciously hear us.

3) Lord, we thank you for the opportunity to learn more of Jesus through his ethos and teaching. Lord hear us.

R. Lord graciously hear us.

The participants may now add their own prayers and petitions. When these prayers and petitions end, there is the recitation of:

The Lord's Prayer

Blessing

May we observe the Beatitudes.

R. Amen.

May we be guided by the Ten Commandments.

R. Amen.

May we opt with the poor.

R. Amen.

And may almighty God bless you, the Father, the Son, and the Holy Spirit.

R. Amen.

Hymn
An appropriate hymn may be sung.

Session 13
Prayer

Opening Prayer
Lord, we place ourselves in your presence. Send us your Spirit to enlighten our minds and open our hearts to your word. We know that Jesus is with us because we are gathered in his name, and he tells us '... where two or three are gathered in my name, I am with them.' We also invite our holy mother Mary, the Seat of Wisdom, to be with us in our sharing. Amen.

Gospel Sharing (Matthew 6:5-15)
This passage highlights the importance of prayer for Jesus. There were thirty hidden years in Nazareth when, 'Jesus increased in wisdom, stature, and in favour with God and men' (Luke 2:2). In those contemplative years this would not have happened without prayer. During the active period of his intense public ministry, Jesus made time to pray. Instances are not far to seek: he prayed and fasted for forty days in the desert immediately before setting out on his mission; before choosing his apostles and delivering his key Sermon on the Mount, '... he [Jesus] went out to the mountain to pray; and he spent the night in prayer to God' (Luke 6:12); following the miracle of the loaves and fishes, he sent his disciples on to Bethsaida at the other side of the lake of Galilee, while he dismissed the crowd. 'After saying farewell to them, he went up on the mountain to pray' (Mark 6:46). He seems to have favoured high places as locales for prayer. Again before his death he prays in the upper room (cf John 17), and in the garden of Gethsemane, where in his agony he sweated blood, he prayed fervently himself and encouraged his disciples to do the same (cf Luke 22:39-46). Praying in the

face of death is no easy matter. I recall a person, in that situation, whom I once encouraged to pray. To which, showing a great understanding of community, he replied, 'I'm so sick I can't pray. Please pray for me.' Prayer in such circumstances shows the value Jesus put on it.

When the disciples, no doubt deeply impressed by the sight of Christ at prayer, asked him to teach them to pray, he introduced them to the Lord's Prayer. In the passage under consideration he says, 'When you are praying, do not heap up empty phrases,' The translation is rather 'don't go blah-blah-blah-blah.' The Greek word 'battalogein' that Matthew uses has the meaning 'blah-blah-blah-blah.' Jesus really didn't use the formal word 'Father', as we understand it. He uses the Aramaic 'Abba' which is like 'papa' and that was probably always the term he used in speaking of God. Indeed 'Abba' is, if anything, even warmer and more intimate than 'papa'. The Lord's Prayer touches all the vital issues: glory and praise of God, will of God, kingdom/realm of God, bread (justice) , forgiveness, deliverance from temptation and evil.

Regarding prayer, it is also essential that it issues in action. Matthew says: 'Not everyone who says to me, "Lord, Lord", will enter the kingdom of heaven, but only the one who does the will of my Father in heaven' (Matthew 7:21).

Jesus tells us not to pile up words when we pray; in fact words aren't even necessary. Charles de Faucauld's definition of prayer is: 'Thinking of God with affection.' No words required there. Prayer is a grace; we can't give it to ourselves. All we can do is dispose ourselves for it and leave the rest to God. If we fail, Paul reminds us that the Spirit within us can pray on our behalf: 'Likewise the Spirit helps us in our weakness; for we do not know how to pray as we ought, but the very Spirit intercedes for us with sighs too deep for words. And God, who searches the heart, knows what is in the mind of the Spirit, for the Spirit intercedes for the saints according to the will of God' (Romans 8:26-27). Sometimes, then, prayer becomes simply waiting patiently in silence. This can be in itself wonderful contemplative prayer; it is the 'waiting on God' practised by saints like Jane de Chantal. Besides, God is not given to brusque intrusion in our lives; God gives us space, God wants us to have space, God respects our space, which is, no doubt, why God chose to be invisible. St Thérèse of Lisieux could not have been more simple in her approach: 'I tell God what I want quite simply, without any splendid turns of phrase, and somehow God always manages to understand me.' Finally, we recall that Jesus encouraged us always to pray and never lose heart (cf Luke 18:1). Prayer was indeed a subject dear to him.

[5]'And whenever you pray, do not be like the hypocrites; for they love to stand and pray in the synagogues and at the street corners, so that they may be seen by others. Truly I tell you they have received their reward. [6]But whenever you pray, go into your room and shut the door and pray to your Father who is in secret, and your Father who sees in secret will reward you.

[7]'When you are praying, do not heap up empty phrases as the Gentiles do, for they think that they will be heard because of their many words. [8]Do not be like them, for your Father knows what you need before you ask him.

[9]'Pray then in this way:

Our Father who are in heaven,

hallowed be your name.

[10]Your kingdom come.

Your will be done, on earth as it is in heaven.

[11]Give us this day our daily bread,

[12]And forgive us our trespasses,
as we forgive those who trespass against us.
[13]And lead us not into temptation,
but deliver us from evil.
[14]For if you forgive others their trespasses, your heavenly Father will also forgive you, but if you do not forgive others, neither will your Father forgive your trespasses.'

Questions
1) What do you learn about Jesus from the foregoing passage?
2) What impressed, questioned, or challenged you in the extract?
3) Taking your own personal experience of Christ into account, does the passage strike any intimate chords for you? *(Because of the nature of this question, it is provided for private rather than group reflection.)*

Reality/Action
How do we put the word of God we have heard into practice? Is there something we can do? Or are we doing something that can be done better? Are there attitudes to change? *(The group should decide on some practical outcome.)*

Spontaneous Prayer
1) With great devotion and attention, the group says 'The Lord's Prayer.'
2) God of mercy, grant that we often think of you with affection, even when no words come. Lord hear us.
R. Lord graciously hear us.

3) God of forgiveness, help us to pardon others readily, and to work patiently to build bridges between ourselves and those from whom we have been separated by hostility. Lord hear us.

R. Lord graciously hear us.

The participants may now add their own prayers and petitions. When these prayers and petitions end, there is the recitation of:

The Lord's Prayer

Random Thoughts
(prior to a cancer operation)
Terror struck within my heart
that morning in early March,
as I waited there for sleep to come,
and helping hands to start.

I thought of the world about me,
in confusion and despair,
nothing left to bargain with,
only the power of prayer.

I said to God be with me,
protect me in my sleep,
raise me to your kingdom,
if these hands do not succeed.

Your prayers for me ascended
like starlets through the mist,
God stretched out a hand to me,
granting your request.

At last I found God's wonder
on that eventful day,
when prayer triumphed in splendour,
and heaven had its way.
(Martin O'Halloran)

More things are wrought by prayer
Than this world dreams of.
(Tennyson)

Blessing
May your name be blessed, O God.
R. Amen.
May your kingdom come.
R. Amen.
May your will be done.
R. Amen.
And may almighty God bless you, the Father, the Son,
and the Holy Spirit.
R. Amen.

Hymn
An appropriate hymn may be sung.

Session 14
The realm of God and its justice

Opening Prayer
Lord, we place ourselves in your presence. Send us your Spirit to enlighten our minds and open our hearts to your word. We know that Jesus is with us because we are gathered in his name, and he tells us '... where two or three are gathered in my name, I am with them.' We also invite our holy mother Mary, the Seat of Wisdom, to be part of our sharing. Amen.

Gospel Sharing (Matthew 6:25-33)
The priority for Jesus is the kingdom, or realm, of God. Many are not happy with the word 'kingdom' that, for them, would have masculine connotations. They would substitute 'reign', which seems to neglect concrete aspects of God's domain. I rather like the term 'realm'; it captures the idea of God's sovereignty and leaves the concrete elements intact. Yet for most of the folk who will use this book 'kingdom' would be the term they will be familiar with. Whatever term we use, the priority for Jesus is the kingdom and its justice. So, of course, it should be the priority for his followers as well. Pope Paul VI describes the kingdom as 'the absolute good' to which everything else must defer (cf The Evangelisation of Peoples, no 8). What is the kingdom then? Briefly it is 'a new creation' (Galatians 6:15) or 'a new heaven and a new earth' (Revelation 21:1); these we must help to create. Again the kingdom is wherever the goodness or graciousness of God breaks through to the world, that is, wherever we find genuine goodness, the kingdom of God is there. It matters not whether the good is being done by Jew or Greek, male or female. The church is part of the kingdom and should

be an effective instrument for building it in the world, yet it is not the whole of the kingdom. Justice (right relationships with ourselves, God, neighbour, and environment) is inseparable from the kingdom, an integral part of Christ's priority. In Matthew 25:31-40, Jesus tells us that whatever is done to even the least of his sisters and brothers, he considers as done to himself. This extract from Matthew 25 is, indeed, the most eloquent plea for justice in the Bible. The following passage also urges us to trust in the providence of God. Finally, the care of the Creator for the environment comes across vividly.

[25]'Therefore I tell you, do not worry about your life, what you will eat or drink, or about your body, what you will wear. Is not life more than food, and the body more than clothing? [26]Look at the birds of the air; they neither sow nor reap nor gather into barns, and yet your heavenly Father feeds them. Are you not of more value than they? [27]And can any of you by worrying add a single hour to your span of life? [28]And why do you worry about clothing? Consider the lilies of the field, how they grow; they toil not, neither do they spin: and [29]yet I say unto you, that even Solomon in all his glory was not arrayed like one of these. [30]But if God so clothes the grass of the fields, which is alive today and tomorrow is thrown into the oven, will he not much more clothe you – you of little faith? [31]Therefore do not worry, saying, "What will we eat?" or "What will we drink?" or "What will we wear?" [32]For it is the Gentiles who strive for all these things; and indeed your heavenly Father knows that you need all these things. [33]But strive first for the kingdom of God and God's justice, and all these things will be given to you as well.'

Questions

1) What do you learn about Jesus from the foregoing passage?

2) What impressed, questioned, or challenged you in the extract?

3) Taking your own personal experience of Christ into account, does the passage strike any intimate chords for you? *(Because of the nature of this question, it is provided for personal rather than group reflection.)*

Reality/Action

How do we put the word of God we have heard into practice? Is there something we can do? Or are we doing something that can be done better? Are there attitudes to change? *(The group should decide on some practical outcome.)*

Spontaneous Prayer

1) God of majesty and power, may your kingdom come; that kingdom for which Christ sacrificed his all. Lord hear us.

R. Lord graciously hear us.

2) Lord, grant that we (the body, hands, and feet of Christ) play our part in building a better world. Lord hear us.

R. Lord graciously hear us.

3) God our provider, Ghandi once said that there is enough in the world for everyone's need, but not for everyone's greed. Help those who have, to share with those who have not. Lord hear us.

R. Lord graciously hear us.

The participants may now add their own prayers and petitions. When these prayers and petitions end, there is the recitation of:

The Lord's Prayer

Blessing
May God's kingdom come.
R. Amen.
May the heavens rain down the Just One.
R. Amen.
May there be bread for everyone's need.
R. Amen.
And may almighty God bless you, the Father, the Son,
and the Holy Spirit.
R. Amen.

Hymn
An appropriate hymn may be sung

Session 15
Do not judge

Opening Prayer
Lord, we place ourselves in your presence. Send us your Spirit to enlighten our minds and open our hearts to your word. We know that Jesus is with us because we are gathered in his name, and he tells us '... where two or three are gathered in my name, I am with them.' We also invite our holy mother Mary, the Seat of Wisdom, to be part of our sharing. Amen.

Gospel Sharing (Matthew 7:1-2)
Jesus asks us not to judge. Only God can truly judge. We cannot fully know another human person; God alone can fathom the depths of the human heart. I cannot even fully know myself. There is the self that I perceive, and there is the self that only God is aware of. We must not make a judgment about seemingly impossible people. Why are they impossible? What circumstance, or even tragedy, in their past makes them so? Such things may not be known to us. Some folk are born into extremely impoverished situations in life; these can be social, emotional, and psychological. They may be even deprived in spiritual and ethical terms. God knows these things and is merciful and compassionate. Judgement, therefore, is best left to God. Indeed, we ought to be immensely relieved that this burden is lifted from our inadequate shoulders.

[1]'Do not judge, so that you may not be judged. [2]For with the judgement you make you will be judged, and the measure you give will be the measure you get.'

Questions
1) What do you learn about Jesus from the foregoing passage?
2) What impressed, questioned, or challenged you in the extract?
3) Taking your personal experience of Christ into account, does the passage strike any intimate chords for you? *(Because of the nature of this question, it is provided for personal rather than group reflection.)*

Reality/Action
How do we put the word of God we have heard into practice? Is there something we can do? Or are we doing something that can be done better? Are there attitudes to change? *(The group should decide on some practical outcome.)*

Spontaneous Prayer
1) God of mercy and compassion, we leave the judgement of ourselves and others in your hands. For only you can fully know us and all the circumstances surrounding our tangled lives. And you alone can plumb the mysterious depths of the human heart. Lord hear us.
R. Lord graciously hear us.
2) God of love, may all our thoughts and actions be prompted by love; otherwise grant that we may not think those thoughts or perform those actions at all. Lord hear us.
R. Lord graciously hear us.
3) Merciful God, being mindful of the harsh lives of so many people, let us not rush to judge or condemn them. Rather let us pity and help them. Lord hear us.
R. Lord graciously hear us.

The participants may now add their own prayers and petitions. When these prayers and petitions end, there is the recitation of:
The Lord's Prayer

Blessing
May we never judge others.
R. Amen.
May we be patient with ourselves.
R. Amen.
May we rely on God alone to judge.
R. Amen.
And may almighty God bless you, the Father, the Son, and the Holy Spirit.
R. Amen.

Hymn
An appropriate hymn may be sung.

Session 16
The rejection of Jesus at Nazareth

Opening Prayer
Lord, we place ourselves in your presence. Send us your Spirit to enlighten our minds and open our hearts to your word. We know Jesus is with us because we are gathered in his name, and he tells us '... where two or three are gathered in my name, I am with them.' We also invite our holy mother Mary, the Seat of Wisdom, to be part of our sharing. Amen.

Gospel Sharing (Luke 4:16-30)
Jesus visited synagogues not just to worship but to teach; it was his custom to go to the synagogue on the sabbath. The sabbath began at sundown on Friday and continued until sundown on Saturday. In vs. 17 and 20 details are given which show us what the procedure was in the synagogue. Jesus stood as he read. At first the people were pleased with his intervention, even took a little local pride in him: 'Is not this Joseph's son?' In the light of what was to follow, this of course may have been somewhat condescending. But when Christ's message begins to sink in, the mood quickly changes to one of rage. He told them that a prophet is not accepted in his own hometown and that foreigners such as the widow of Zarephath in Sidon and Naaman the Syrian knew God's help when Israel did not. The problem in Nazareth was that Jesus could not work miracles there as he had in Capernaum, because the Nazarenes were lacking in faith. Such was their fury that they wanted to kill him. This rejection by his own townsfolk must have been devastating for Jesus. We all experience rejections in life and know that there is nothing more painful, especially when they involve people

who are dear to us. As far as we know, he never again visited Nazareth. One of the most significant things about this passage is that Jesus makes a graphic mission statement (vs. 18-19): his is a clear option with the poor and oppressed. This meant being in solidarity with them, identifying with their problems, adopting a simple lifestyle, and reaching out towards them to love and share. There was nothing patronising or diminishing in his approach.

16When he came to Nazareth, where he had been brought up, he went to the synagogue on the sabbath day, as was his custom. He stood up to read, 17and the scroll of the prophet Isaiah was given. He unrolled the scroll and found the place where it was written:

18'The Spirit of the Lord is upon me,

because he has anointed me

to bring good news to the poor.

He has sent me to proclaim release to the captives

and recovery of sight to the blind,

to let the oppressed go free,

19to proclaim the year of the Lord's favour.'

20And he rolled up the scroll, gave it back to the attendant, and sat down. The eyes of all in the synagogue were fixed on him. 21Then he began to say to them, 'Today this scripture has been fulfilled in your hearing.' 22All spoke well of him and were amazed at the gracious words that came from his mouth. They said, 'Is not this Joseph's son?' 23He said to them, 'Doubtless you will quote me this proverb, "Doctor cure yourself!" And you will say, "Do here also in your hometown the things that we have heard you did in Capernaum".' 24And he said, 'Truly I tell you, no prophet is accepted in the prophet's hometown. 25But the truth is, there were many widows in Israel in the time of Elijah, when the heavens were shut up for three years and six months, and there was a severe famine over all the land; 26yet Elijah was sent to none of them except to a widow in Zarephath in Sidon. 27There were also many lepers in Israel in the time of the prophet Elisha, and none of them was cleaned except Naaman the Syrian.' 28When they heard this, all in the synagogue were filled with rage. 29They got up, drove him out of town, and led him to the brow of the hill on which their town was built, so that they might hurl him off the cliff. 30But he passed through the midst of them and went on his way.

Questions
1) What do you learn about Jesus from the foregoing passage?
2) What impressed, questioned, or challenged you in the extract?
3) Taking your personal experience of Christ into account, does the passage strike any intimate chords for you? *(Because of the nature of this question, it is provided for personal rather than group reflection.)*

Reality/Action
How do we put the word of God we have heard into practice? Is there something we can do? Or are we doing something that can be done better? Are there attitudes to change? *(The group should decide on some practical outcome.)*

Spontaneous Prayer
1) Lord, faith makes all things possible. Increase our faith. Lord hear us.
R. Lord graciously hear us.

2) Ever faithful God, when we suffer rejection by those whom we love, may we remember that Christ himself endured the same. Strengthen, console, and heal us. Lord hear us.

R. Lord graciously hear us.

3) God of the little ones, may we make Jesus' clear option with the poor our own. Lord hear us.

R. Lord graciously hear us.

The participants may now add their own prayers and petitions. When these prayers and petitions end, there is the recitation of:

The Lord's Prayer

Blessing

May we believe totally in Christ.

R. Amen.

May we cope with rejection.

R. Amen.

May we opt for the little ones of our world.

R. Amen.

And may almighty God bless you, the Father, the Son. and the Holy Spirit.

R. Amen.

Hymn

An appropriate hymn may be sung.

Session 17
The one who is to come

Opening Prayer
Lord, we place ourselves in your presence. Send us your
Spirit to enlighten our minds and open our hearts to
your word. We know Jesus is with us because we are
gathered in his name, and he tells us '... where two or
three are gathered in my name, I am with them.' We
also invite our holy mother Mary, the Seat of Wisdom,
to be part of our sharing. Amen.

Gospel Sharing (Matthew 11:1-6)
*As Jesus preached in the cities of Galilee, an imprisoned
John the Baptist sent his disciples to ask if he was the
Messiah, the eagerly awaited leader and saviour of Israel.
At the Baptism of Jesus, John already seemed to recognise
this, so why is he asking the question? Some writers have
said that John asked this question for his disciples rather
than for himself. He wanted to confirm their faith in
Jesus. More likely, he shared in such perplexity as we
sometimes find in Jesus himself, and genuinely wished to
know. Jesus answers as best he can by telling the disciples
to go tell John what they hear and see. The items he lists
were deeds that Isaiah said would be performed by the
Messiah (cf Isaiah 29:18-19; 35:5-6; 61:1). In effect
Jesus was asking John to look at the fruits. Earlier, he had
indicated this as an infallible way of divining spirits: 'By
their fruits you shall know them' (Matthew 7:20). The
deeds listed by Jesus speak volumes about the concerns of
Christ. The first verse of the passage makes an interesting
point. Before going out to the multitudes, Jesus first finished instructing his disciples. Throughout his ministry
we find him trying to balance these two things. On the*

one hand, he devotes much time to the reduced group of
disciples. This shows the importance of basic communities
and ferment groups. Yet he does not neglect the mass of
the people either: 'I have compassion on the multitude,'
he tells us in Matthew 15:32 (cf also Mark 8:2).

[1]Now when Jesus had finished instructing his twelve
disciples, he went on from there to teach and proclaim
his message in the cities.

[2]When John heard in prison what the Messiah was
doing, he sent word by his disciples [3]and said to him,
'Are you the one who is to come, or are we to wait for
another?' [4]Jesus answered them, 'Go tell John what
you hear and see: [5]the blind receive their sight, the
lame walk, the lepers are cleansed, the deaf hear, the
dead are raised, and the poor have the good news
brought to them. [6]And blessed is anyone who takes no
offence at me.'

Questions

1) What do you learn about Jesus from the foregoing
passage?

2) What impressed, questioned, or challenged you in
the extract?

3) Taking your personal experience of Christ into
account, does the passage strike any intimate chords
for you? *(Because of the nature of this question, it is pro-*
vided for personal rather than group reflection.)

Reality/Action

How do we put the word of God we have heard into
practice? Is there something we can do? Or are we
doing something that can be done better? Are there
attitudes to change? *(The group should decide on some*
practical outcome.)

Spontaneous Prayer

1) God of wisdom, be with us in our moments of perplexity. May your Spirit guide our feet along the right path even when the way ahead is not entirely clear. Lord hear us.

R. Lord graciously hear us.

2) Lord, help us to avail of that wonderful gospel maxim: By their fruits you shall know them. It is a sure compass for navigating the stormy seas of life. Lord hear us.

R. Lord graciously hear us.

3) Caring God, while we appreciate the absolute necessity of reduced groups and communities and diligently attend to them, let us not fail to have compassion on the multitude. May we serve the mass of God's people equally well. Lord hear us.

R. Lord graciously hear us.

The participants may now add their own prayers and petitions. When these prayers and petitions end, there is the recitation of:

The Lord's Prayer

Blessing

May the Messiah be praised.

R. Amen.

May we be known by our fruits.

R. Amen

May all God's people experience compassion.

R. Amen.

And may almighty God bless you, the Father, the Son, and the Holy Spirit.

R. Amen.

Hymn
An appropriate hymn may be sung.

Session 18
The Samaritan Woman

Opening Prayer
Lord, we place ourselves in your presence. Send us your Spirit to enlighten our minds and open our hearts to your word. We know Jesus is with us because we are gathered in his name, and he tells us '… where two or three are gathered in my name, I am with them.' We also invite our holy mother Mary, the Seat of Wisdom, to he part of our sharing. Amen.

Gospel Sharing (John 4:7-30, 39-42)
On his way from Judea to Galilee, a tired out Jesus stops by the well of Shechem/Sychar in Samaria and asks the Samaritan woman for a drink. There occurs a most fascinating encounter between the two. Ignoring rebuffs and efforts to tie him up in various issues between Jews and Samaritans, Jesus steadily confronts her with the faith issue, until in the end she is thoroughly convinced and converted. Indeed the transformation was so complete that she became an apostle to her own city, leading the people to Jesus. If we understand 'apostle' as one who is sent with a purpose and is available for this, then she was a legitimate apostle. Apostles aren't confined to the original twelve. Jesus' openness to the Samaritan woman is impressive; most Jews would ignore her, and rabbis were not supposed to speak to women in public. Besides, Jews generally held Samaritans in contempt as apostates (cf 2 Kings 17:24-34). They did not worship in Jerusalem but on Mount Gerizim; they were in fact despised as spurious worshippers of the true God. Further they were the descendants of a doubtful mixture of Israelites and people from various Mesopotamian communities who had been

settled in Israel. With the conversions in this story John is making the point that Samaritans came into community alongside Jews. Even more obvious is the issue of replacement (how one reality replaces another). Here worship in the temple is replaced by worship in spirit and in truth; it's a matter of heart and soul primarily and not of buildings. Then we have the more adequate faith of these strangers replacing the less adequate faith of those in Jerusalem (John 2:23-25) and of Nicodemus. It is worth noting that by ' living water' Jesus means 'abundant life.' The woman calls Jesus a prophet, the implication being that he should be able to provide a true answer to such questions as to whether Mount Gerizim or Jerusalem was the legitimate place of worship. Finally, Jesus being tired out when he arrives at the well shows us his humanity; in general, however, it is the divinity of Christ that John is keen on emphasising. The drama of the encounter with the Samaritan women tells us much about Jesus.

[7] A Samaritan woman came to draw water, and Jesus said to her, 'Give me a drink.' [8] (His disciples had gone to the city to buy food.) [9] The Samaritan woman said to him, 'How is it that you, a Jew, ask a drink of me, a woman of Samaria?' (Jews do not share things in common with Samaritans.) [10] Jesus answered her, 'If you knew the gift of God, and who it is that is saying to you, "Give me a drink", you would have asked him, and he would have given you living water.' [11] The woman said to him, 'Sir, you have no bucket, and the well is deep. Where do you get that living water? [12] Are you greater than our ancestor Jacob, who gave us the well, and with his sons and his flocks drank from it?' [13] Jesus said to her, 'Everyone who drinks of this water will be thirsty again, [14] but those who drink of the water that I will give them will never be thirsty. The water that I will give will become in them a spring of

water gushing up to eternal life.' 15The woman said to him, 'Sir, give me this water, so that I may never be thirsty or have to keep coming here to draw water.'

16Jesus said to her, 'Go call your husband and come back.' 17The woman answered him, 'I have no husband.' Jesus said to her. 'You are right in saying, "I have no husband"; 18for you have had five husbands, and the one you have now is not your husband. What you have said is true!' 19The woman said to him, 'Sir, I see that you are a prophet. 20Our ancestors worshipped on this mountain, but you say that the place where people must worship is in Jerusalem.' 21Jesus said to her, 'Woman, believe me, the hour is coming when you will worship the Father neither on this mountain nor in Jerusalem. 22You worship what you do not know; we worship what we know, for salvation is from the Jews. 23But the hour is coming, and is now here, when the true worshippers will worship the Father in spirit and truth, for the Father seeks such as these to worship him. 24God is spirit, and those who worship him must worship in spirit and truth.' 25The woman said to him, 'I know that the Messiah is coming' (who is called Christ). 'When he comes, he will proclaim all things to us.' 26Jesus said to her, 'I am he, the one who is speaking to you.'

27Just then his disciples came. They were astonished that he was speaking with a woman, but no one said, 'What do you want?' or 'Why are you speaking with her?' 28Then the woman left her water jar and went back to the city. She said to the people, 29'Come and see a man who told me everything I have ever done! He cannot be the Messiah, can he?' 30They left the city and were on their way to him ...

39Many Samaritans from that city believed in him

because of the woman's testimony, 'He told me everything I have ever done.' [40]So when the Samaritans
came to him, they asked him to stay with them; and
he stayed there two days. [41]And many more believed
because of his word. [42]They said to the woman , 'It is
no longer because of what you have said that we
believe, for we have heard for ourselves, and we know
that this is truly the Saviour of the world.'

Questions
1) What do you learn about Jesus from the foregoing
passage?
2) What impressed, questioned, or challenged you in
the extract?
3) Taking your personal experience of Christ into
account, does the passage strike any intimate chords
for you? *(Because of the nature of this question, it is provided for personal rather than group reflection.)*

Reality/Action
How do we put the word of God we have heard into
practice? Is there something we can do? Or are we
doing something that can be done better? Are there
attitudes to change? *(The group should decide on some
practical outcome.)*

Spontaneous Prayer
1) God of all peoples, grant that, like Jesus, we may
look into our hearts and never find there the possibility of rejecting anyone because they are different. Lord
hear us.
R. Lord graciously hear us.
2) Zealous God, may we answer the call to be true
apostles as did the Samaritan woman. Lord hear us.
R. Lord graciously hear us.

3) Gracious God, we thirst. Give us the living water of abundant life. Lord hear us.

R. Lord graciously hear us.

The participants may now add their own prayers and petitions. When these prayers and petitions end, there is the recitation of:

The Lord's Prayer

Blessing

May we rejoice in diversity.

R. Amen.

May we have the zeal of the apostle.

R. Amen.

May we always enjoy the living water.

R. Amen,

And may almighty God bless you, the Father, the Son, and the Holy Spirit.

R. Amen.

Hymn

An appropriate hymn may be sung.

Session 19
The Eucharist

Opening Prayer

Lord, we place ourselves in your presence. Send us your Spirit to enlighten our minds and open our hearts to your word. We know Jesus is with us because we are gathered in his name, and he tells us '... where two or three are gathered in my name, I am with them.' We also invite our holy mother Mary, the Seat of Wisdom, to be with us in our sharing. Amen.

Gospel Sharing (John 6:35-58)

John does not give an account of the eucharist at the Lord's Supper. But this passage related to Jesus' ministry in Galilee is obviously about eucharist. A vague Christian spirituality unrelated to practice is not enough; we must eat the flesh of the Son of Man and drink his blood. Jesus himself became flesh and thereby soiled his hands in this world. Christianity too must be involved with the planet; it is about feeding the hungry, giving drink to the thirsty, eating the flesh and drinking the blood of Christ. And if we eat the same flesh and drink the same blood, how can we be other than united? Jesus generously breaks bread with the whole world and we are challenged to do the same. This profoundly questions an unbridled capitalism, for example, that engenders hunger, disease, and exclusion on our planet. In short, it is not Christian. Jesus' act of sharing is symbolic and is not simply about sharing materially; it entails sharing vision, faith, ideas and friendship as well. Through the eucharist Jesus has devised an ingenious means of being with us always. Sanctuary lamps glow red by tabernacles all over the world, even in the most remote corners. The word 'eucharist' means 'thanksgiving.' In the passage, not surprisingly, John hones in on Jesus' divinity; he is the Son, the one who has come down from heaven. Interesting how Jesus' listeners tended to dismiss him because he was the son of Joseph and Mary. It is a human trait not to appreciate the worth of someone who is familiar to us, especially when they make good. In Ireland we all know the force of a statement like, 'I knew him when he didn't have a seat in his trousers!'

35Jesus said to them, 'I am the bread of life. Whoever comes to me will never be hungry, and whoever believes in me will never be thirsty. 36But I said to you that you have seen me and yet do not believe. 37Everything that the Father gives me will come to me, and anyone who comes to me I will never drive away; 38for I have come down from heaven, not to do my own will, but the will of him who sent me. 39And this is the will of him who sent me, that I should lose nothing of all that he has given me, but raise it up on the last day. 40This is indeed the will of my Father, that all who see the Son and believe in him may have eternal life, and I will raise them up on the last day.'

41Then the Jews began to complain about him because he said, 'I am the bread that came down from heaven.' 42They were saying, 'Is not this Jesus, the son of Joseph, whose father and mother we know? How can he now say, "I have come down from heaven?"' 43Jesus answered them, 'Do not complain among yourselves. 44No one can come to me unless drawn by the Father who sent me; and I will raise that person up on the last day. 45It is written in the prophets, "And they shall be taught by God." Everyone who has heard and learned from the Father comes to me. And this is the will of him who sent me. 46Not that anyone has seen the Father except the one who is from God; that person has seen the Father. [47]Very truly, I tell you, whoever believes has eternal life. [48]I am the bread of life. [49]Your ancestors ate manna in the wilderness, and they died. [50]This is the bread that comes down from heaven, so that one may eat of it and not die. [51]I am the living bread that came down from heaven. Whoever eats of this bread will live forever; and the bread that I will give for the life of the world is my flesh.

[52]The Jews disputed among themselves saying, 'How can this man give us his flesh to eat?' [53]So Jesus said to them, 'Very truly I tell you, unless you eat the flesh of the Son of Man and drink his blood, you have no life in you. [54]Those who eat my flesh and drink my blood have eternal life and I will raise them up on the last day; [55]for my flesh is true food and my blood is true drink. [56]Those who eat my flesh and drink my blood abide in me, and I in them. [57]Just as the living Father sent me, and I live because of the Father, so whoever eats me will live because of me. [58]This is the bread that came down from heaven, not like that which our ancestors ate, and died. But the one who eats this bread will live forever.' [59]He said these things while he was teaching in the synagogue at Capernaum.

Questions
1) What do you learn about Jesus from the foregoing passage?
2) What impressed, questioned, or challenged you in the extract?
3) Taking your personal experience of Christ into account, does the passage strike any intimate chords for you? *(Because of the nature of this question, it is provided for personal rather than group reflection.)*

Reality/Action

How do we put the word of God we have heard into practice? Is there something we can do? Or are we doing something that can be done better? Are there attitudes to change? *(The group should decide on some practical outcome.)*

Spontaneous Prayer

1) Lord, give us the bread of life, so that we may never be hungry again. And may we believe in you, so that we will not thirst. Lord hear us

R. Lord graciously hear us.

2) Bountiful God, because of our life in Jesus, may we eat the bread of eternal life and so be raised up on the last day. Lord hear us.

R. Lord graciously hear us.

3) God of wisdom, may we recognise Christ, when he comes our way, and not be blinded by prejudice. For the ragged, even troublesome, beggar at our doors is Christ. Lord hear us.

R. Lord graciously hear us.

The participants may now add their own prayers and petitions. When the prayers and petitions end, there is the recitation of:

The Lord's Prayer

Blessing
May we never lack the bread of life.
R. Amen.
May our faith never falter.
R. Amen.
May we always recognise Christ.
R. Amen.
And may almighty God bless you, the Father, the Son,
and the Holy Spirit.
R. Amen.

Hymn
An appropriate hymn may be sung.

Session 20
The woman caught in adultery

Opening Prayer
Lord, we place ourselves in your presence. Send us your Spirit to enlighten our minds and open our hearts to your word. We know Jesus is with us, because we are gathered in his name, and he tells us '... where two or three are gathered in my name, I am with them.' We also invite our holy mother Mary, the Seat of Wisdom, to be part of our sharing. Amen.

Gospel Sharing (John 8:1-11)
In this passage, John is again at his dramatic best. The atmosphere is nail-biting as the fate of the woman hangs in the balance and Jesus deals with the trap that the scribes and Pharisees have set for him. The resolution is brilliant. According to several later manuscripts, what Jesus wrote on the ground was the sins of the woman's accusers. That scattered them! The passage is very revealing of Christ and of God, because Jesus is, of course, a human way of being divine. So what is true of him is also true of God. The obvious attributes are mercy and compassion, but other qualities are in evidence too. Though Jesus is kindness personified, he is nevertheless firm and enjoins the woman not to sin again. With God's grace she can do this. Incidentally, where is the man that was involved in this adultery? Since the woman was caught in the act, so too was he. That he seems to have been able to escape the dire consequences tells us much of the status of women in Jewish society at the time.

Then each of them went home, ¹while Jesus went to the Mount of Olives. ²Early in the morning he came again to the temple. All the people came to him and sat down and he began to teach them. ³The scribes and the Pharisees brought a woman who had been caught in adultery; and making her stand before all of them, ⁴they said to him, 'Teacher, this woman was caught in the very act of committing adultery. ⁵Now in the law Moses commanded us to stone such women. Now what do you say?' ⁶They said this to test him, so that they might have some charge to bring against him. Jesus bent down and wrote with his finger on the ground. ⁷When they kept on questioning him, he straightened up and said to them, 'Let anyone among you who is without sin be the first to throw a stone at her.' ⁸And once again he bent down and wrote on the ground. ⁹When they heard it, they went away, one by one, beginning with the elders; and Jesus was left alone with the woman standing before him. ¹⁰Jesus straightened up and said to her, 'Woman, where are they? Has no one condemned you?' ¹¹She said, 'No one, sir.' And Jesus said, 'Neither do I condemn you. Go your way, and from now on do not sin again.'

Questions

1) What do you learn about Jesus from the foregoing passage?

2) What impressed, questioned, or challenged you in the extract?

3) Taking your personal experience of Christ into account, does the passage strike any intimate chords for you? (*Because of the nature of this question, it is provided for personal rather than group reflection.*)

Reality/Action

How do we put the word of God we have heard into practice? Is there something we can do? Or are we doing something that can be done better? Are there attitudes to change? *(The group should decide on some practical outcome.)*

Spontaneous Prayer

1) God of mercy and compassion, may we appreciate the gift of Jesus whose treatment of the woman taken in adultery mirrors your own infinite mercy and compassion. He is the key to knowing you. Lord hear us.

R. Lord graciously hear us.

2) Gracious God, may we imitate the sorrow and humility which brought forgiveness to the hapless woman. Lord hear us.

R. Lord graciously hear us.

3) God of wisdom, may your Spirit guide us when we are called upon to make decisions in seemingly catch 22 situations. Lord hear us.

R. Lord graciously hear us.

4) God of justice, may we be fair to all people irrespective of religion, race, sex, or colour. Lord hear us.

R. Lord graciously hear us.

The participants may now add their own prayers and petitions. When these prayers and petitions end, there is the recitation of:

The Lord's Prayer

Blessing
May the God of mercy be praised.
R. Amen.
May the God of compassion be honoured.
R. Amen.
May Jesus, the compassion of God, be glorified.
R. Amen.
And may almighty God bless you, the Father, the Son,
and the Holy Spirit.
R. Amen.

Hymn
A suitable hymn may be sung.

Session 21
The Canaanite woman's faith

Opening Prayer

Lord, we place ourselves in your presence. Send us your Spirit to enlighten our minds and open our hearts to your word. We know Jesus is with us, because we are gathered in his name, and he tells us '... where two or three are gathered in my name, I am with them.' We also invite our holy mother Mary, the Seat of Wisdom, to be part of our sharing. Amen.

Gospel Sharing (Matthew 15:21-28)

Jesus went in a northwesterly direction from upper Galilee into Phoenicia, the district of Tyre and Sidon. He was, therefore, outside of Israel. Here the Canaanite woman implores him to heal her daughter, who has a demon. Interestingly, the woman addresses Jesus as the Jewish Messiah, calling him 'Lord, Son of David.' Jesus does not reply to her request. He is in a quandary; his understanding of his mission is that he is sent to the lost sheep of the house of Israel, and here is a foreigner seeking his help. She recognises his mission, yet appeals to him as a gentile. Because of her great faith, he responds and heals her daughter. Her faith is the deciding factor; the Spirit was undeniably at work in her. Had he not said himself, 'You will know them by their fruits' (Matthew 7:16)? Despite perplexity around his identity and mission, Christ responds to faith wherever it is found. The story is remarkably similar to the healing of the Roman centurion's servant boy (Matthew 8:5-13). Again, despite limitations that he believes are placed upon him, Jesus is, at a cost, open to the stranger. In every age, there are limitations of time and place within which we have to

*move and work. Nevertheless, if we do our best, God's
purposes are achieved. Further Christ functions as a healer,
as he does so often in the gospels. 'Dog' in scripture is a
derogatory term. The comparison that Jesus apparently
makes of gentiles to dogs seems extremely harsh to modern
ears. In a Near Eastern context it would have been much
less so. 'The dialogue is an instance of the kind of wit that
was and is admired in the Near East, the same wit that
is called wisdom in the Old Testament; it is the ability to
match riddle with riddle, to cap one wise saying with
another, to match insult with insult, or – as here – to
turn the insult into a commitment ... Jesus would not
have been a genuine Palestinian if he had not occasion-
ally engaged in a duel of wit. The scene is much more a
scene of peasant good humour than it is of solemn theological debate' (The Jerome Biblical Commentary). The
outcome is an indication that not only did Christ appreciate the woman's faith, but also her wit.*

21Jesus left that place, and went away to the district of
Tyre and Sidon. 22Just then a Canaanite woman from
the region came out and started shouting, 'Have
mercy on me, Lord, Son of David; my daughter is
tormented by a demon.' 23But he did not answer her
at all. And his disciples came and urged him, saying,
'Send her away, because she keeps shouting after us.'
24He answered, 'I was sent only to the lost sheep of the
house of Israel.' 25But she came and knelt before him,
saying, 'Lord, help me.' 26He answered, 'It is not fair
to take the children's food and throw it to the dogs.'
27She said, 'Yes, Lord, yet even the dogs eat the
crumbs that fall from the master's table.' 28Then Jesus
answered her, 'Woman, great is your faith! Let it be
done for you as you wish.' And her daughter was
healed instantly.

Questions
1) What do you learn about Jesus from the foregoing passage?
2) What impressed, questioned, or challenged you in the extract?
3) Taking your personal experience of Christ into account, does the passage strike any intimate chords for you? *(Because of the nature of this question, it is provided for personal rather than group reflection.)*

Reality/Action
How do we put the word of God we have heard into practice? Is there something we can do? Or are we doing something that can be done better? Are there attitudes to change? *(The group should decide on some practical outcome.)*

Spontaneous Prayer
1) God of all peoples, even when it is extremely difficult, may we be open to the stranger and those who are different, as your Son Jesus was. Lord hear us.
R. Lord graciously hear us.
2) God of abundant life, give us health of mind and body, and may we, like Jesus, be healers of body, heart, and mind. Lord hear us.
R. Lord graciously hear us.
3) Lord, give us a modicum of the faith that the Canaanite woman had, as she loudly pleaded for the health of her child. And may we too find a witty response when we need to. Lord hear us.
R. Lord graciously hear us.
The participants may now add their own prayers and petitions. When these prayers and petitions end, there is the recitation of:
The Lord's Prayer

Blessing
May we be open to the stranger and those who are different.
R. Amen.
With the help of the Spirit may we decide bravely when this is called for.
R. Amen.
May we mend broken bodies and broken hearts.
R. Amen.
And may almighty God bless you, the Father, the Son, and the Holy Spirit.
R. Amen.

Hymn
An appropriate hymn may be sung.

Session 22
'But who do you say that I am?'

Opening Prayer

Lord, we place ourselves in your presence. Send us your Spirit to enlighten our minds and open our hearts to your word. We know Jesus is with us because we are gathered in his name and he tells us '... where two or three are gathered in my name, I am with them.' We also invite our holy mother Mary, the Seat of Wisdom, to be with us in our sharing. Amen.

Gospel Sharing (Matthew 16:13-20, 22)

Jesus asks the apostles, 'But who do you say that I am?' Peter answers unequivocally, 'You are the Messiah, the Son of the living God.' Jesus is pleasantly surprised, because he recognises that only God could make a spiritual disclosure of this magnitude. It couldn't have come from Peter himself. The keys of the kingdom are a symbol of power; Jesus makes Peter a leader of the church. Power in Jesus' eyes would be totally different from what often passes for power in the world; not power as status, but power as a means to service. Jesus' decision to go to Jerusalem is regarded as a defining moment in his ministry, indeed in his life.

In the gospels, Christ often makes 'I am' statements, or declarations of his identity, particularly in the gospel of John. We quote them below, so that they may be teased out and reflected upon. Perhaps a couple of examples will facilitate the process:

• 'I am the bread of life' (John 6:35). Jesus here compares himself to bread. Bread sustains life, nourishes, satisfies, causes celebration, fosters relationships when shared, and can be a powerful instrument for justice. Above all, using

bread and wine, Christ gave us his flesh to eat and his blood to drink, and, through bread thus transformed, lives with us always ... and so on.

• *'I am the Good Shepherd' (John 10:11). A good shepherd or shepherdess protects the sheep, cleanses them, medicates them, leads them to rich pastures, seeks them out when they are lost; they also know their animals intimately, call them, lead them, even talk to them, though they may only get a bleat in reply ... and so forth.*

13Now when Jesus came into the district of Caesarea Philippi, he asked the disciples, 'Who do people say that the Son of Man is?' 14And they said, 'Some say John the Baptist, but others Elijah, and still others Jeremiah or one of the prophets.' 15He said to them, 'but who do you say that I am?' 16Simon Peter answered, 'You are the Messiah, the Son of the living God.' 17And Jesus answered him, 'Blessed are you Simon, Son of Jonah! For flesh and blood has not revealed this to you, but my Father in heaven. 18And I tell you, you are Peter, and on this rock I will build my church and the gates of Hades will not prevail against it. 19I will give you the keys of the kingdom of heaven, and whatever you bind on earth will be bound in heaven, and whatever you loose on earth will be loosed in heaven.' 20Then he sternly ordered his disciples not to tell anyone that he was the Messiah.

22From that time on, Jesus began to show his disciples that he must go to Jerusalem and undergo great suffering at the hands of the elders and chief priests and scribes, and be killed, and on the third day be raised.

'I am' statements from Jesus himself:
• I am the bread of life (John 6:35).
• I am the light of the world (John 8:12).
• I am not from this world (John 8:23).

- I am he (John 8:24).
- I am the gate for the sheep (John 10:7).
- I am the Good Shepherd (John 10:11).
- I am the resurrection and the life (John 11:25).
- I am who I am (John 13:19).
- I am the way, the truth, and the life (John 14:16).
- I am the real vine (John 15:1).

Questions
1) What do you learn about Jesus from the foregoing passages?
2) What impressed, questioned, or challenged you in the extracts?
3) Taking your personal experience of Christ into account, does the passage strike any intimate chords for you? *(Because of the nature of this question, it is provided for personal rather than group reflection.)*

Reality/Action
How do we put the word of God we have heard into practice? Is there something we can do? Or are we doing something that can be done better? Are there attitudes to change? *(The group should decide on some practical outcome.)*

Spontaneous Prayer
1) Lord of truth, to Jesus' question for the disciples, 'Who do you say that I am?' we too give the resounding answer, 'You are the Messiah, the Son of the living God.' Lord hear us.
R. Lord graciously hear us.
2) God of Wisdom, teach us to understand that power gets its force, not from domination, but from service. Lord hear us.
R. Lord graciously hear us.

3) God of strength, give us the willpower to face our destiny with the determination which Christ showed when he courageously set his face towards Jerusalem, despite the cruel fate that awaited him there. Lord hear us.

R. Lord graciously hear us.

The participants may now add their own prayers and petitions. When these prayers and petitions end, there is the recitation of:

The Lord's Prayer

Blessing

May we follow Jesus the way.

R. Amen.

May we find Jesus the truth.

R. Amen.

May we experience Jesus the life.

R. Amen.

And may almighty God bless you, the Father, the Son, and the Holy Spirit.

R. Amen.

Hymn

An appropriate hymn may be sung.

Session 23
Jesus transfigured

Opening Prayer

Lord, we place ourselves in your presence. Send us your Spirit to enlighten our minds and open our hearts to your word. We know Jesus is with us, because we are gathered in his name, and he tells us '... where two or three are gathered in my name, I am with them.' We also invite our holy mother Mary, the Seat of Wisdom, to be part of our sharing. Amen.

Gospel Sharing (Matthew 17:1-9)

The main point Matthew wishes to communicate is that Jesus is the beloved Son of God. Jesus' face shining like the sun reminds us of the face of Moses on encountering God on Mount Sinai. As we have seen, Matthew, who worked with a mixed community of Jews and gentiles, likes to find parallels for his account of proceedings in the Old Testament. The transfiguration somehow strongly anticipates Jesus' resurrection. Focus is also put prophetically on the role of Peter who of his own accord offers to build three dwellings on the mountain: one for Jesus, one for Moses, and one for Elijah. When Christ tells the apostles not to be afraid, he is saying something that he repeated on a number of occasions in the gospels. He is obviously acutely aware of this all too human trait and wants us to take these consoling words to heart. Peter is so happy on the mountain that he is disposed to stay there forever. But Jesus takes him back to the humdrum existence of every day; life is not totally about exalted experiences. The technical term for what happened at the transfiguration is a 'theophany', or a visible manifestation of God to humans. I also believe it is a Trinitarian event. The voice

*of the Father and the gleaming figure of Jesus, the Son,
are obvious; I feel the bright, overshadowing cloud is symbolic of the Spirit. We think of Mary being overshadowed
by the Spirit at the incarnation. So there is the heavenly
community of Father, Son, and Spirit together with
Moses and Elijah, and the earthly community of Jesus,
Peter, James, and John. Jesus is the mediator between
both communities.*

[1]Six days later, Jesus took with him Peter and James
and his brother John and led them up a high mountain, by themselves. [2]And he was transfigured before
them, and his face shone like the sun, and his clothes
became dazzling white. [3]Suddenly there appeared to
them Moses and Elijah, talking with them. [4]Then
Peter said to Jesus, 'Lord, it is good for us to be here;
if you wish, I will make three dwellings here, one for
you, one for Moses, and one for Elijah.' [5]While he was
still speaking, suddenly a bright cloud overshadowed
them, and from the cloud the voice said, 'This is my
Son, the Beloved; with him I am well pleased; listen to
him!' [6]When the disciples heard this, they fell to the
ground and were overcome by fear. [7]But Jesus came
and touched them saying, 'Get up and do not be
afraid.' [8]And when they looked up, they saw no one
but Jesus himself alone.

[9]As they were coming down the mountain, Jesus
ordered them, 'Tell no one about the vision until after
the Son of Man has been raised from the dead.'

Questions

1) What do you learn about Jesus from the foregoing
passage?
2) What impressed, questioned, or challenged you in
the extract?

3) Taking your personal experience of Christ into account, does the passage strike any intimate chords for you? *(Because of the nature of this question, it is provided for personal rather than group reflection.)*

Reality/Action

How do we put the word of God we have heard into practice? Is there something we can do? Or are we doing something that can be done better? Are there attitudes to change? *(The group should decide on some practical outcome.)*

Spontaneous Prayer

1) God of majesty and power, we adore and thank you for the gift of your Son, the Beloved. Grant that we hear him, for he alone has the word of everlasting life. Lord hear us.

R. Lord graciously hear us.

2) Eternal God, may we realise that life is not easy and that the best way to deal with this is to get usefully involved. Help us to do so. Lord hear us.

R. Lord graciously hear us.

3) God rich in mercy, may your love grow within us in such a way that all fear is banished from our hearts. Lord hear us.

R. Lord graciously hear us.

The participants may now add their own prayers and petitions. When these prayers and petitions end, there is the recitation of:

The Lord's Prayer

Blessing
May God in the highest be glorified.
R. Amen.
May God's Son, the Beloved, be ever honoured.
R. Amen.
May all fear be banished from our hearts.
R. Amen
And may almighty God bless you, the Father, the Son,
and the Holy Spirit.
R. Amen.

Hymn
An appropriate hymn may be sung.

Session 24
The Good Samaritan

Opening Prayer
Lord, we place ourselves in your presence. Send us your Spirit to enlighten our minds and open our hearts to your word. We know Jesus is with us, because we are gathered in his name, and he tells us '... where two or three are gathered in my name, I am with them.' We also invite our holy mother Mary, the Seat of Wisdom, to be part of our sharing. Amen.

Gospel Sharing (Luke 10:29-37)
The questioner in this passage is a lawyer who has just asked Jesus what he should do to gain eternal life. Jesus in turn asked him what was written in the law, and he replied, 'You shall love the Lord your God with all your heart, and with all your soul, and with all your strength, and with all your mind; and your neighbour as yourself.' Jesus said, 'You have given the right answer, do this, and you will live.' The lawyer, of course, has accurately stated the The Great Commandment. Loving all, unconditionally, is indeed a high ethic. However, with God's grace it can be done and is, in fact, the most practical way to approach life. It was what Jesus the consummate human being did, and he knew what was best. If we grasp the nettle, we will surely find that it is so. The questioning lawyer wanted to show his right to eternal life by describing what his duty was, and showing how he had fulfilled it. So to be precise about the matter of what this duty consisted and desiring to show himself to be acceptable, he asked, 'And who is my neighbour?' To answer Jesus tells the parable of the Good Samaritan. The interesting thing about this story is that it is not about an indeterminate

man; it is specifically about a Samaritan, and, therefore, in Jewish eyes an enemy and a stranger. Every fictional story is autobiographical, so this one will tell us much about Christ. It certainly provides an eloquent answer to the question posed. Every human being is our neighbour and we must love them, even if they consider themselves our enemy. Jesus' ethos is not a matter of loving friends. This presents no problem. His mandate also embraces enemies. This is the point of the parable. Both the priest, who represented the highest religious authority among the Jews, and the levite, the lay associate of the priest, failed to help their fellow countryman. It was a despised Samaritan who was moved with pity. His was a genuine love. As so often happens in the gospel, goodness is found in unexpected places. And isn't that only too true of life? Oil and wine were frequently used as ancient medicines.

29But wanting to justify himself, he asked Jesus, 'And who is my neighbour?' 30Jesus replied, 'A man was going down from Jerusalem to Jericho, and fell into the hands of robbers, who stripped him, beat him, and went away, leaving him half dead. 31Now by chance a priest was going down that road; and when he saw him, he passed by on the other side. 32So likewise a Levite, when he came to the place and saw him, passed by on the other side. 33But a Samaritan while travelling came near to him; and when he saw him, he was moved with pity. 34He went to him and bandaged his wounds, having poured oil and wine on them. Then he put him on his own animal, brought him to an inn, and took care of him. 35The next day he took out two denarii, gave them to the innkeeper, and said, "Take care of him; and when I come back, I will repay you whatever more you spend." 36Which of these three, do you think, was neighbour to the man that fell into the hands of the robbers?' 37He said, 'The one who showed him mercy.' Jesus said to him, 'Go and do likewise.'

Questions

1) What do you learn about Jesus from the foregoing passage?
2) What impressed, questioned, or challenged you in the extract?
3) Taking your personal experience of Christ into account, does the passage strike any intimate chords for you? *(Because of the nature of this question, it is provided for personal rather than group reflection.)*

Reality/Action

How do we put the word of God we have heard into practice? Is there something we can do? Or are we doing something that can be done better? Are there attitudes to change? *(The group should decide on some practical outcome.)*

Spontaneous Prayer

1) God of surprises, you continually push out the boundaries. If we think we are doing well when we love friends and people of our race, then the impressive story of the Good Samaritan challenges us to think again. May we be open to, and love, every human being irrespective of race, nation, social condition, religion, gender, or age. Lord hear us.
R. Lord graciously hear us.
2) God of the unexpected, help us to appreciate goodness when it comes from unexpected people and unexpected places. Lord hear us.
R. Lord graciously hear us.

3) Healing God, when we encounter folk with wounds of mind or body, let us pour soothing oil and wine on those wounds and never rub salt into them. Lord hear us.

R. Lord graciously hear us.

The participants may now add their own prayers and petitions. When these prayers and petitions end, there is the recitation of:

The Lord's Prayer

Blessing

May we love God and all God's people.

R. Amen.

May we love all other living creatures.

R. Amen

May we love all of creation.

R. Amen.

And may almighty God bless you, the Father, the Son, and the Holy Spirit.

R. Amen..

Hymn

An appropriate hymn may be sung.

Session 25
The Prodigal Son

Opening Prayer
Lord, we place ourselves in your presence. Send us your Spirit to enlighten our minds and open our hearts to your word. We know Jesus is with us, because we are gathered in his name, and he tells us '… where two or three are gathered in my name, I am with them.' We also invite our holy mother Mary, the Seat of Wisdom, to be with us in our sharing. Amen.

Gospel Sharing (Luke 15:11-32)
Through this parable Jesus is highlighting the qualities he admires in God. Needless to say the qualities that are found in God are the same as those found in Jesus himself. When on one occasion the apostle Philip asked Christ to show 'us' the Father, he replied, 'Whoever has seen me has seen the Father' (John 14:9). He could have added 'and the Spirit'. However, the parable does show us the characteristics in God that impress Jesus, which is interesting. As already mentioned, Jesus' stories are quite revealing, because they are inevitably autobiographical. The love and forgiveness of the father in the parable are amazing; they could transform our image of God. The parent rushes out to greet his wayward son, and forgives him even before he delivers his rehearsed little speech to humiliate himself and ask for pardon. The father didn't need the speech; he had read the body language and seen into the sinner's heart. The old man rushing out to embrace and kiss the prodigal possibly looked silly. Yet in his delight he didn't care. He is totally selfless, and contrasts sharply with the self-centred elder brother, who doesn't seem even to begin to understand what love is

about. It is sad to see him so dismissive of his wonderful father and repentant brother with a snide remark like 'this son of yours'. The expression is countered by the father's referring to the prodigal as 'this brother of yours' in his reply. Even at his most wayward, the prodigal son was probably never more distant from God than his smug elder brother. Just a few final details: to herd pigs would have been an utter indignity for a Jew; the robe put on the prodigal was a festive one, not to be worn while working; the ring was a symbol of authority; and the sandals too were significant, for slaves went unshod.

[11]Then Jesus said, 'There was a man who had two sons. [12]The younger of them said to his father, "Father, give me the share of the property that will belong to me." So he divided his property between them. [13]A few days later the younger son gathered all he had and travelled to a distant country, and there he squandered his property in dissolute living. [14]When he had spent everything, a severe famine took place throughout that country, and he began to be in need. [15]So he went and hired himself out to one of the citizens of that country, who sent him to his fields to feed pigs. [16]He would gladly have filled himself with the pods that the pigs were eating; and no one gave him anything. [17]But when he came to himself he said, "How many of my fathers's hired hands have bread enough and to spare, but here I am dying of hunger! [18]I will get up and go to my father, and I will say to him, 'Father, I have sinned against heaven and against you; [19]I am no longer worthy to be called your son; treat me like one of your hired hands.'" [20]So he set off and went to his father. But while he was still far off, his father saw him and was filled with compassion; he ran and put his arms around him and kissed him. [21]Then the son said to him, "Father, I have sinned

against heaven and before you. I am no longer worthy to be called your son." ²²But the father said to his slaves, "Quickly, bring out a robe – the best one – and put it on him; put a ring on his finger and sandals on his feet. ²³And get the fatted calf and kill it, and let us eat and celebrate; ²⁴for this son of mine was dead and is alive again; he was lost and is found!" And they began to celebrate.

²⁵'Now his elder son was in the field; and when he came and approached the house, he heard music and dancing. ²⁶He called one of the slaves and asked what was going on. ²⁷He replied, "Your brother has come, and your father has killed the fatted calf, because he has got him back safe and sound." ²⁸Then he became angry and refused to go in. His father came out and began to plead with him. ²⁹But he answered his father, "Listen! For all these years I have been working like a slave for you, and I have never disobeyed your command; yet you have never given me even a young goat so that I might celebrate with my friends. ³⁰But when this son of yours came back, who has devoured your property with prostitutes, you killed the fatted calf for him!" ³¹Then the father said to him, "Son, you are always with me, and all that is mine is yours. ³²But we had to celebrate and rejoice, because this brother of yours was dead and has come to life; he was lost and has been found."'

Questions
1) What do you learn about Jesus from the foregoing passage?
2) What impressed, questioned, or challenged you in the extract?

3) Taking your personal experience of Christ into account, does the passage strike any intimate chords for you? *(Because of the nature of this question, it is provided for personal rather than group reflection.)*

Reality/Action
How do we put the word of God we have heard into practice? Is there something we can do? Or are we doing something that can be done better? Are there attitudes to change? *(The group should decide on some practical outcome.)*

Spontaneous Prayer
1) Bountiful God, your mercy and compassion are endless. May we never despair of your mercy, or fail to avail of your compassion. Lord hear us.
R. Lord graciously hear us.
2) Lord, your divine Son Jesus is rightly named the compassion of God, a compassion that led our Saviour to console and heal us; indeed ultimately to die for us. Grant that we never cease to treasure that compassion. Lord hear us.
R. Lord graciously hear us.
3) God of forgiveness, may we never doubt that, no matter how often we fall, when there is genuine sorrow and repentance, you always pardon. Jesus showed us that this is so. Lord hear us.
R. Lord graciously hear us.
The participants may now add their own prayers and petitions. When these prayers and petitions end, there is the recitation of:
The Lord's Prayer

Blessing
May we be merciful.
R. Amen.
May we be compassionate.
R. Amen.
May we be forgiving.
R. Amen.
And may almighty God bless you, the Father, the Son,
and the Holy Spirit.
R. Amen.

Hymn
An appropriate hymn may be sung.

Session 26
He came to serve

Opening Prayer
Lord we place ourselves in your presence. Send us your Spirit to enlighten our minds and open our hearts to your word. We know that Jesus is with us because we are gathered in his name, and he tells us, '... where two or three are gathered in my name, I am with them.' We also invite our holy mother Mary, the Seat of Wisdom, to be part of our sharing. Amen.

Gospel Sharing (Matthew 20:20-28)
Jesus here turns the worldly idea of leadership on its head. The leader's role is one of animation, co-ordination, facilitation, enablement, service, not domination. And the way forward in the church is through dialogue and consensus. So important is this message that it is found in Matthew, Mark, and Luke substantially as below. We don't find the reading in John, but we have the washing of the apostles' feet (John 13), which makes the same point. So leadership is not about being above or below people, but working shoulder to shoulder with them in community. Perhaps we should speak of it as a 'ministry' of service to community, just as there are other such ministries: for liturgy, youth, music, prisoners, the sick, and so forth. These gifts are no less estimable than an ability for animation/co-ordination in which leadership consists. Unfortunately, for thousands of years leadership has been seen as a matter of domination. The fact that this reading is found in the three synoptic gospels (Matthew, Mark, Luke) goes to show that Jesus certainly uttered these words or something quite close to them. The notion of the Suffering Servant who gives his life as a ransom for others is to be found in Isaiah 53.

20Then the mother of the sons of Zebedee came to him with her sons, and kneeling before him, she asked a favour of him. 21And he said to her, 'What do you want?' She said to him, 'Declare that these two sons of mine will sit, one at your right hand and the other at your left, in your kingdom.' 22But Jesus answered, 'You do not know what you are asking. Are you able to drink the cup that I am about to drink?' They said to him, 'We are able.' 23He said to them, 'You will indeed drink my cup, but to sit at my right hand and at my left, this is not mine to grant, but it is for those for whom it has been prepared by my Father.'

24When the ten heard it, they were angry with the two brothers. 25But Jesus called them to him and said, 'The rulers of the Gentiles lord it over them, and their great ones are tyrants over them. 26It will not be so among you; but whoever wishes to be great among you must be your servant, 27and whoever wishes to be first among you must be your slave; 28just as the Son of Man came not to be served but to serve, and to give his life as a ransom for many.'

Questions

1) What do you learn about Jesus from the foregoing passage?

2) What impressed, questioned, or challenged you in the extract?

3) Taking your personal experience of Christ into account, does the passage strike any intimate chords for you? *(Because of the nature of this question, it is provided for personal rather than group reflection.)*

Reality/Action

How do we put the word of God we have heard into practice? Is there something we can do? Or are we doing something that can be done better? Are there attitudes to change? *(The group should decide on some practical outcome.)*

Spontaneous Prayer

1) God of service, imbue us with the truth that real leadership is about service and not a matter of lording it over people 'as the gentiles do'. Jesus became man, not to be served, but to serve. Let us, his disciples, imitate him in this. Lord hear us.

R. Lord graciously hear us.

2) Sensitive God, may we be lovers of dialogue and deeply respectful of the views of others. Above all, assist us in being good listeners. Lord hear us.

R. Lord graciously hear us.

3) Lord, help us always to look for consensus, while, at the same time, being attentive to the prophetic voices that challenge us. Lord hear us.

R. Lord graciously hear us.

The participants may now add their own prayers and petitions. When these prayers and petitions end, there is the recitation of:

The Lord's Prayer

Blessing
May we be servants.
R. Amen,
May we not dominate.
R. Amen.
May we imitate the meekness of Christ.
R. Amen.
And may almighty God bless you, the Father, the Son,
and the Holy Spirit.
R. Amen.

Hymn
An appropriate hymn may be sung.

Session 27
Raising of Lazarus

Opening Prayer
Lord, we place ourselves in your presence. Send us your Spirit to enlighten our minds and open our hearts to your word. We know Jesus is with us, because we are gathered in his name, and he tells us, 'where two or three are gathered in my name, I am with them.' We also invite our holy mother Mary, the Seat of Wisdom, to be with us in our sharing. Amen.

Gospel Sharing (John 11:1-7, 17-45)
Jesus gives life to Lazarus, even as he gave light to the blind man; in doing so he performs the greatest of his signs. The strange irony is that this led to the decision of the Sanhedrin that he must die (John 11:45-53). In the dialogue before the miracle, Martha acknowledges that Jesus is the Messiah, the Son of God. This confession of faith can be compared with Peter's renowned one (Matthew 16:16), and it came earlier! It also reminds us of the most significant confession of faith made in the gospels, that of Thomas (cf John 20:29). Martha also believes that her brother will arise on the last day. Jesus, however, leads her to an even deeper faith. Not only is Christ the resurrection, but also the life, and whoever believes in him will never die. Jesus doesn't only raise from the dead on the last day; he gives life now. Lazarus was raised, yet that was only a sign, for he will die one day. This was symbolised by his coming forth from the tomb still bound in burial robes. Jesus comes to give eternal life, impervious to death, so, when he rises, he leaves his shroud in the sepulchre. The Jews had elaborate burial ceremonies and many attended. Ten persons, at least,

were required to take part in them, and they went on for thirty days. They believed that the soul lingered near the body for three days and then left. So Lazarus, being four days in the tomb, was definitely dead. Again on this occasion, Martha is the active person, Mary meditative, as happened in Luke 10:38-42. They both show disappointment, saying that if Jesus had been present, their brother would not have died. Nevertheless they are not without hope 'even now.' Martha expressly says so. 'Asleep' is often used for 'death' in the New Testament. In the passage, as one would expect, John is emphasising the fact that Jesus is divine, the one sent by God. Nevertheless the humanity of Christ is highlighted in this episode. He is indignant at death for having removed his friend and distressed the sisters, who were of course also dear friends. His sorrow leads him to weep openly. 'See how he loved him,' the onlookers declared. Like ourselves, Jesus is a vulnerable human being. We saw it when he was rejected at Nazareth, for example, and again when he wept inconsolably over Jerusalem. How blessed we are to have Jesus for a friend, because that is what he considers us: 'You are my friends if you do what I command you. I do not call you servants any longer, because the servant does not know what the master is doing; but I have called you friends, because I have made known to you everything that I have heard from my Father' (John 15:14-15).

[1]Now a certain man was ill, Lazarus of Bethany, the village of Mary and her sister Martha. [2]Mary was the one who anointed the Lord with perfume and wiped his feet with her hair; her brother Lazarus was ill. [3]So the sisters sent a message to Jesus, 'Lord, he whom you love is ill.' [4]But when Jesus heard it he said, 'This illness does not lead to death; rather is it for God's glory, so that the Son of God may be glorified through it.' [5]Accordingly, though Jesus loved Martha and her sister

and Lazarus, [6]after having heard that Lazarus was ill, he stayed two days longer in the place where he was. [7]Then after this he said to the disciples, 'Let us go to Judea again ...'

[17]When Jesus arrived, he found that Lazarus had already been in the tomb four days. [18]Now Bethany was near Jerusalem, some two miles away, [19]and many of the Jews had come to Martha and Mary to console them about their brother. [20]When Martha heard that Jesus was coming, she went and met him, while Mary stayed at home. [21]Martha said to Jesus, 'Lord, if you had been here my brother would not have died. [22]But even now I know that God will give you whatever you ask for.' [23]Jesus said to her, 'Your brother will rise again.' [24]Martha said to him, 'I know that he will rise again in the resurrection on the last day.' [25]Jesus said to her, 'I am the resurrection and the life. Those who believe in me, even though they die, will live, [26]and everyone who lives and believes in me will never die. Do you believe this?' [27]She said to him, 'Yes, Lord, I believe that you are the Messiah, the Son of God, the one coming into the world.'

[28]When Jesus had said this, she went back and called her sister Mary, and told her privately, 'The Teacher is here and is calling for you.' [29]And when she heard it, she got up quickly and went to him. [30]Now Jesus had not yet come to the village, but was still at the place where Martha had met him. [31]The Jews who were with her in the house, consoling her, saw Mary get up quickly and go out. They followed her because they thought she was going to the tomb to weep there. [32]When Mary came where Jesus was and saw him, she knelt at his feet and said to him, 'Lord, if you had been here, my brother would not have died,' [33]When

Jesus saw her weeping, and the Jews who had come with her also weeping, he was greatly disturbed in spirit and deeply moved. ³⁴He said, 'Where have you laid him?' They said to him, 'Lord come and see.' ³⁵Jesus began to weep. ³⁶So the Jews said, 'See how he loved him.' ³⁷But some of them said, 'Could not he who opened the eyes of the blind man have kept this man from dying.'

³⁸Then Jesus, again greatly disturbed, came to the tomb. It was a cave and a stone was lying against it. ³⁹Jesus said, 'Take away the stone,' Martha, the sister of the dead man, said to him. 'Lord already there is a stench because he has been dead four days.' ⁴⁰Jesus said to her, 'Did I not tell you that if you believed, you would see the glory of God?' ⁴¹So they took away the stone. And Jesus looked upward and said, 'Father, I thank you for having heard me. ⁴²I knew that you always hear me, but I have said this for the sake of the crowd standing here, so that they may believe that you sent me.' ⁴³When he had said this, he cried out with a loud voice, 'Lazarus, come out!' ⁴⁴The dead man came out, his hands and feet bound with strips of cloth, and his face wrapped in cloth. Jesus said to them, 'Unbind him, and let him go.'

⁴⁵Many of the Jews, therefore, who had come with Mary and had seen what Jesus did, believed in him.

Questions
1) What do you learn about Jesus from the foregoing passage?
2) What impressed, questioned, or challenged you in the extract?

3) Taking your own personal experience of Christ into account, does the passage strike any intimate chords for you? *(Because of the nature of this question, it is provided for personal rather than group reflection.)*

Reality/Action

How do we put the word of God we have heard into practice? Is there something we can do? Or are we doing something that can be done better? Are there attitudes to change? *(The group should decide on some practical outcome.)*

Spontaneous Prayer

1) Living God, you have given us your Son Jesus who is the resurrection and the life. Not only does he hold out the possibility of our rising from the dead, but by conquering death assures us that we will live forever. Through him, may we also rise to live eternally. Lord hear us.
R. Lord graciously hear us.

2) Lord God, John is at pains to point to Jesus' divinity and, indeed, only one who is divine has power over life and death. We adore you, O Christ, and we bless you, because by your holy cross you have redeemed the world. Lord hear us.
R. Lord graciously hear us.

3) Lord of heaven and earth, we are in awe at your Son becoming a vulnerable human being like ourselves. How moving to see him driven to tears on behalf of those he loves; how admirable to know he is such a tender and faithful friend because, as we learn from John 15:15, he calls us friends too. Lord hear us.
R. Lord graciously hear us.

The participants may now add their own prayers and petitions. When these prayers and petitions end, there is the recitation of:
The Lord's Prayer

Blessing
May God the Creator of all life be praised.
R. Amen.
May Christ the resurrection and the life be glorified.
R. Amen.
May we cherish the rich humanity of Jesus.
R. Amen.
And may almighty God bless you, the Father, the Son, and the Holy Spirit.
R. Amen.

Hymn
An appropriate hymn may be sung.

Endings
– and New Dawn

Session 28
One in Christ

Opening Prayer

Lord, we place ourselves in your presence. Send us your Spirit to enlighten our minds and open our hearts to your word. We know that Jesus is with us because we are gathered in his name, and he tells us '... where two or three are gathered in my name, I am with them.' We also invite our holy mother Mary, the Seat of Wisdom, to be with us in our sharing. Amen.

Gospel Sharing (John 17:20-26)

Jesus' heartfelt plea in this passage is 'that they may all be one'. John, the great theologian of community, seizes on what Christ has to say and unfolds his stupendous Trinitarian vision. The Father, the Son, and the Holy Spirit, though three distinct persons, are one God, or one Community. God is community, and we are created in the image and likeness of God (cf Genesis 1:26-27), so we too must be community. Though various persons, through our loving and sharing, we become one community and so are like the Trinity. This intimate relationship can, of course, only fully take place in small, or basic, communities; these then combine in greater assemblies, such as that of the parish, to form the communion of communities. For a full experience of church we need the intimate group and, beyond that, the communion of communities. The vision John articulates here of church as community in the image of the Trinity is the same model proposed by Vatican II (cf Paragraph 4 in the 'Dogmatic Constitution on the Church'), a model now in the making on every continent. Jesus' burning desire that his followers be one is among his last, most urgent and most moving prayers. He is to die on the morrow. It is vital that his followers be one, otherwise no one is going to believe in his gospel of love. The extract is obviously relevant for ecumenism, or the manner in which we reach out to other Christian denominations and other religions. By giving each other an experience of authentic love, we provide an experience of God who is love, and become channels of God's love for one another. Just to note that for John the word 'glory' has the same meaning as 'love'; also we note that in the scriptures 'world' is used in two senses – to describe God's wonderful creation, but also to describe the world of sin. We must judge from the context; in this passage we find it used in both senses. The way John struggles with words makes us aware of how inadequate human language is to deal with deep mystery.

[20]'I ask not only on behalf of these, but also on behalf of those who will believe in me through their word, [21]that they may all be one. As you Father are in me and I am in you, may they also be in us, so that the world may believe that you have sent me. [22]The glory that you have given me I have given them, so that they may be one, as we are one. [23]I in them and you in me, that they may be completely one, so that the world may know that you have sent me and have loved them even as you have loved me. [24]Father, I desire that those also, whom you have given me, may be with me where I am, to see my glory, which you have given me because you loved me before the foundation of the world.

[25]'Righteous Father, the world does not know you, but I know you; and these know that you have sent me. [26]I made your name known to them, and I will make it

known, so that the love with which you loved me may
be in them, and I in them.'

Questions
1) What do you learn about Jesus from the foregoing
passage?
2) What impressed, questioned, or challenged you in
the extract?
3) Taking your personal experience of Christ into
account, does the passage strike any intimate chords
for you? *(Because of the nature of this question, it is provided for personal rather than group reflection.)*

Reality/Action
How do we put the word of God we have heard into
practice? Is there something we can do? or are we
doing something that can be done better? Are there
attitudes to change? *(The group should decide on some
practical outcome.)*

Spontaneous Prayer
1) God of tenderness, may we heed the ardent prayer
of Jesus that we be one as the Father, the Son, and the
Spirit are one, so that people may believe in the good
news of the gospel. Lord hear us.
R. Lord graciously hear us.
2) God most generous, grant that we be always deeply
moved and grateful that your Son remembered to pray
especially for us on a night of such anguish and suffering for himself. Lord hear us.
R. Lord graciously hear us.
3) Likewise may we appreciate his saying something
that shows real affection for ourselves. Lord hear us.
R. Lord graciously hear us.

4) Lord, we earnestly beseech you that the church be a community in the image of the Trinity. Lord hear us.
R. Lord graciously hear us.

The participants may now add their own prayers and petitions. When these prayers and petitions end, there is the recitation of:
The Lord's Prayer

Blessing
May we all be one.
R. Amen.
May we pray for others as Jesus prayed for us.
R. Amen.
May we love others with the affection Jesus has for us.
R. Amen
And may almighty God bless you, the Father, the Son, and the Holy Spirit.
R. Amen.

Hymn
An appropriate hymn may be sung.

Session 29
The death of Christ

Opening Prayer
Lord, we place ourselves in your presence. Send us your
Spirit to enlighten our minds and open our hearts to
your word. We know Jesus is with us because we are
gathered in his name and he tells us '... where two or
three are gathered in my name, I am with them.' We
also invite our holy mother Mary, the Seat of Wisdom,
to be part of our sharing. Amen.

Gospel Sharing (Matthew 27:45-54)
*As at the birth of Jesus, gentiles once more recognise him
as the Son of God in death. There was the star when Jesus
was born, and here there are dire happenings in nature at
his passing, happenings which point to the end times. The
veil of the temple is rent in two, the old order is gone. The
children of Israel are raised from the dead, the new era has
begun. The ominous events bring home to us the enormity of what has occurred: we have killed our Saviour. If we
want to know how much God loves us and how God cares
for us, then we can do no better than look at the dead
Christ. The cross is the most eloquent symbol of God's
compassion for us. Jesus' cry, 'My God, my God, why have
you forsaken me?' is heart-rending. This is not theatre; he
really does feel abandoned by God and is tempted to
despair. But he does not succumb to despair. As he goes
through the gap of death, he clings on with his fingernails,
hoping and trusting in his God and in the promise of the
kingdom. That kingdom which he had so eloquently pro-
claimed along the winding ways of Palestine. And God
did not fail him. By raising him from the dead the Lord
put the seal of approval on this man's life and on the kingdom he had preached. Did God really want the blood of*

his beloved Son? It is an intriguing question best answered perhaps by another. Could it be that the cross is what we did to Jesus, and the raising from the dead what God did? Never does Jesus look so vulnerable and so powerless as in his passing. He is truly human. Did he fully grasp his own divinity? How could one who was human do so? Yet the centurion and those with him had no doubt about Christ's divine credentials and declared in awe, 'Indeed this was the Son of God.' Matthew is kindly to Romans in his gospel, possibly because he dealt with a mixed community of Jews and gentiles at Antioch. The cosmopolitan Luke, who probably worked with the churches founded by Paul, is, if anything, kinder still to Romans.

[45]From noon on, darkness came over the whole land until three in the afternoon. [46]And about three o'clock Jesus cried out with a loud voice, 'Eli, Eli, lema sabachthani?' that is, 'My God, my God, why have you forsaken me.' [47]When some of the bystanders heard it they said, 'This man is calling for Elijah.' [48]At once one of them ran and got a sponge, filled it with sour wine, put it on a stick, and gave it to him to drink. [49]But the others said, 'Wait, let us see whether Elijah will come and save him.' [50]Then Jesus cried again with a loud voice and breathed his last. [51]At that moment the curtain of the temple was torn in two, from top to bottom. The earth shook and the rocks were split. [52]The tombs also were opened, and many bodies of the saints who had fallen asleep were raised. [53]After his resurrection they came out of the tombs and entered the holy city and appeared to many. [54]Now when the centurion and those with him, who were keeping watch over Jesus, saw the earthquake and what took place, they were terrified and said, 'Indeed this was the Son of God.'

Questions
1) What do you learn about Jesus from the foregoing passage?
2) What impressed, questioned, or challenged you in the extract?
3) Taking your personal experience of Christ into account, does the passage strike any intimate chords for you? *(Because of the nature of this question, it is provided for personal rather than group reflection.)*

Reality/Action
How do we put the word of God we have heard into practice? Is there something we can do? Or are we doing something that can be done better? Are there attitudes to change? *(The group should decide on some practical outcome.)*

Spontaneous Prayer
1) God of our salvation, the dire signs that accompanied the death of Jesus remind us of the enormity of what happened. How we crucified your only begotten Son. Lord, from the depths of our being we ask for pardon and, with your assistance, promise not to crucify the Saviour anew through our sins. Lord hear us.
R. Lord graciously hear us.
2) God of majesty and power, crucifixion is what we did to Jesus; what you did was to raise him to life. We praise and glorify you for your goodness. Lord hear us.
R. Lord graciously hear us.
3) Lord, we thank you without ceasing for having sent Jesus as our Saviour. Lord hear us.
R. Lord graciously hear us.

The participants may now add their own prayers and petitions. When these prayers and petitions end, there is the recitation of:
The Lord's Prayer

Blessing
May the Father of the Saviour be praised.
R. Amen.
May the Son be blessed.
R. Amen.
May the Spirit fill our hearts with a longing for the salvation so dearly bought.
R. Amen.
And may Almighty God bless you, the Father, the Son, and the Holy Spirit.
R. Amen.

Hymn
An appropriate hymn may be sung.

Session 30
Resurrection

Opening Prayer
Lord, we place ourselves in your presence. Send us your
Spirit to enlighten our minds and open our hearts to
your word. We know Jesus is with us because we are
gathered in his name, and he tells us '... where two or
three are gathered in my name, I am with them.' We
also invite our holy mother Mary, the Seat of Wisdom,
to be part of our sharing. Amen.

Gospel Sharing (Matthew 28:1-10)
*The tomb is empty! Jesus is risen from the dead! The
Resurrection, as Paul reminds us, is the greatest and most
significant mystery of our faith. If Christ had not risen,
our faith would be in vain; the whole story would have
ended sadly at his death. Yet it doesn't; it now goes on forever, for Christ has conquered death. Furthermore, not
only does he live forever, but holds out the prize of everlasting life to all of us. And he is still with us through his
church, which is his body. Not surprisingly there is no figure in history who makes the impact he does. The role of
the women in the Resurrection story is noteworthy. They
are the first witnesses to it, and being a witness to the
Resurrection is considered one of the main attributes of
the foundational apostle. Notice Jesus' injunction that the
women should not be afraid. It is a note constantly
sounded in the gospels. If God loves us, why be afraid?*
[1]After the sabbath, as the first day of the week was
dawning, Mary Magdalene and the other Mary went
to the tomb. [2]And suddenly there was a great earthquake; for an angel of the Lord, descending from
heaven, came and rolled back the stone and sat on it.

[3]His appearance was like lightning, and his clothing white as snow. [4]For fear of him the guards shook and became like dead men. [5]But the angel said to the women, 'Do not be afraid; I know you are looking for Jesus who was crucified. [6]He is not here; for he has been raised as he said. Come, see the place where he lay. [7]Then go quickly and tell his disciples. "He has been raised from the dead and indeed he is going ahead of you to Galilee; there you will see him." This is my message for you.' [8]So they left the tomb quickly and with great joy, and ran to tell his disciples. [9]Suddenly Jesus met them and said, 'Greetings!' And they came to him, took hold of his feet, and worshipped him. [10]Then Jesus said to them, 'Do not be afraid; go tell my brothers to go to Galilee; there they will see me.'

Questions

1) What do you learn about Jesus from the foregoing passage?

2) What impressed, questioned, or challenged you in the extract?

3) Taking your personal experience of Christ into account, does the passage strike any intimate chords for you? *(Because of the nature of this question, it is provided for personal rather than group reflection.)*

Reality/Action

How do we put the word of God we have heard into practice? Is there something we can do? Or are we doing something that can be done better? Are there attitudes to change? *(The group should decide on some practical outcome.)*

Spontaneous Prayer

1) God of majesty and glory, we can only fall at the feet of the risen Christ and adore him, as the holy women did. Because of the Resurrection, we believe with all our hearts. May we never fail to thank you, Lord, for raising up your Son and setting the seal of approval on all his endeavours. Lord hear us.

R. Lord graciously hear us.

2) God of mercy, just as Jesus rose from the dead, so too will we. May we rise to be with you, and all those we love, forever in paradise. Lord hear us.

R. Lord graciously hear us.

3) Lord may we be effective witnesses to the Resurrection as were the holy women. Lord hear us.

R. Lord graciously hear us.

4) Gracious God, grant that the fire of your infinite love may burn all fear from our hearts. Lord hear us.

R. Lord, graciously hear us.

The participants may now add their own prayers and petitions. When these prayers and petitions end, there is the recitation of:

The Lord's Prayer

The Resurrection
(Johann Greither's painting)
Down a cloud of light,
picking his steps, dances
the Saviour, kicking out
death's door, emerging
with all the abandon
of someone with nothing
to fear; one suspects
the balancing arms
and skipping feet – head tossed
in the air – will continue
to baffle script writers
and military men.
(Hugh O'Donnell)

'... why look for the living among the dead?'
— *Luke 24:5*

Blessing
May we be truly a risen people.
R. Amen.
May we, like Jesus, rise to glory.
R. Amen.
May we be faithful witnesses to the risen Christ.
R. Amen.
And may almighty God bless you, the Father, the Son,
and the Holy Spirit.
R. Amen.

Hymn
An appropriate hymn may be sung.

Session 31
The road to Emmaus

Opening Prayer

Lord, we place ourselves in your presence. Send us your Spirit to enlighten our minds and open our hearts to your word. We know that Jesus is with us because we are gathered in his name, and he tells us '… where two or three are gathered in my name, I am with them.' We also invite our holy mother Mary, the Seat of Wisdom, to be part of our sharing. Amen.

Gospel Sharing (Luke 24:13-33)

Luke likes to have Jesus talk with his disciples on long journeys – it shortens the road. It was the same on the long journey to Jerusalem, where he went to die. The two disciples in this story saw Jesus, but somehow they didn't recognise him. After all, his body at this stage was a transformed body, so the difficulty may have lain there. Significantly, they eventually recognised him in the breaking of the bread. God is love, Jesus is divine, they recognise him in an act of sharing, or of love. When Christ joined the two disciples, they were utterly depressed over the recent happenings in Jerusalem. To make matters worse some women, who had visited the tomb, came back saying that Jesus had risen from the dead. At that stage these two disciples must have said something like, 'We're out of here!' and set off for a walk in the country to clear their heads. Jesus surely felt sorry for them and set about the task of restoring their spirits. It was necessary that Jesus should suffer, and the Father accepted his sacrifice and drew good from it. As Jesus explains, Moses and all the prophets had foretold it would be so. It wasn't that God wanted the death of his

*Son, but the prophetic stances that Christ took in his
ministry led inevitably to the cross. The Emmaus story is
well told. Luke demonstrates his dramatic flair. There is
the tension all the way through created by the disciples
not recognising Christ. It's Jesus! Why, oh why can't they
recognise him? They just carried on with their heads
down, one imagines, caught up in their miseries.
However, what the stranger was saying was somehow reg-
istering. Later, having recognised the Lord, they declared
that their hearts burned within them as he spoke to them
on the road. Another clever device was Jesus making as if
to continue on his journey, when the two men reached
their destination. It's Jesus! Don't let him go! To our great
relief, they didn't. Then there comes the marvellous
moment of recognition, and immediately he vanishes
from their sight, leaving them astounded.*

[13]Now on that same day two of them were going to a
village called Emmaus, about seven miles from
Jerusalem, [14]and talking with each other about all
these things that had happened. [15]While they were
talking and discussing, Jesus came near and went with
them, [16]but their eyes were kept from recognising
him. [17]And he said to them, 'What are you discussing
with each other while you walk along?' They stood
still, looking sad. [18]Then one of them, whose name
was Cleopas, answered him, 'Are you the only stranger
in Jerusalem who does not know the things that have
taken place there in these days?' [19]He asked them,
'What things?' They replied, 'The things about Jesus
of Nazareth who was a prophet mighty in deed and
word before God and all the people, [20]and how our
chief priests and leaders handed him over to be condemned to death and crucified him. [21]But we had
hoped that he was the one to redeem Israel. Yes, and
besides all this, it is now the third day since all these

things took place. 22Moreover, some women of our group astounded us. They were at the tomb early this morning, 23and when they did not find his body there, they came back and told us that they had indeed seen a vision of angels who said that he was alive. 24Some of those who were with us went out to the tomb and found it was just as the women had said but they did not see him.' 25Then he said to them, 'Oh, how foolish you are, and how slow of heart to believe all that the prophets have declared! 26Was it not necessary that the Messiah should suffer these things and then enter into his glory?' 27Then beginning with Moses and all the prophets, he interpreted to them the things about himself in all the scriptures.

28As they came near the village to which they were going, he walked ahead as if he were going on. 29But they urged him strongly saying, 'Stay with us, because it is almost evening and the day is now nearly over.' So he went in to stay with them. 30When he was at the table with them, he took bread, blessed and broke it, and gave it to them. 31Then their eyes were opened, and they recognised him; and he vanished from their sight. 32They said to each other, 'Were not our hearts burning within us while he was talking to us on the road, while he was opening the scriptures to us?' 33That same hour they got up and returned to Jerusalem.

Questions
1) What do you learn about Jesus from the foregoing passage?
2) What impressed, questioned, or challenged you in the extract?

3) Taking your personal experience of Christ into account, does the passage strike any intimate chords for you? *(Because of the nature of this question, it is provided for personal rather than group reflection.)*

Reality/Action

How do we put the word of God we have heard into practice? Is there something we can do? Or are we doing something that can be done better? Are there attitudes to change? *(The group should decide on some practical outcome.)*

Spontaneous Prayer

1) God of wisdom, grant that we walk with Jesus in life and, on that journey, learn from him. Lord hear us.

R. Lord graciously hear us.

2) Loving God, make our hearts burn within us as we listen to the words of Jesus, and assist us in putting those words into practice daily. Lord hear us.

R. Lord graciously hear us.

3) Lord, may we break bread with others and may they recognise the God of love in our act of sharing. Lord hear us.

R. Lord graciously hear us.

The participants may now add their own prayers and petitions. When these prayers and petitions end, there is the recitation of:

The Lord's Prayer

Blessing
May we ever walk with Jesus.
R. Amen.
May his words warm our hearts.
R. Amen.
May we break bread with others.
R. Amen.
And may almighty God bless you, the Father, the Son,
and the Holy Spirit.
R. Amen,

Hymn
An appropriate hymn may be sung.

Session 32
Peter summarises the Christ event

Opening Prayer
Lord, we place ourselves in your presence. Send us your
Spirit to enlighten our minds and open our hearts to
your word. We know that Jesus is with us because we
are gathered in his name, and he tells us, '... where two
or three are gathered in my name, I am with them.'
We also invite our holy Mother Mary, the Seat of
Wisdom, to be part of our sharing. Amen.

Scripture Sharing (Acts 2:14-42)
*The context of the following passage is the Jewish Feast of
Pentecost. Pentecost meaning 'fiftieth day' was an important Hebrew festival. A harvest celebration, it was held
fifty days after the Passover and recalled the liberation of
the Jews from Egypt under the leadership of Moses. This
particular celebration coincided with the descent of the
Holy Spirit upon Mary and the disciples, which led to
Pentecost being adopted by the Christian church as an
important feast. Having just received, and being filled
with the Holy Spirit the disciples seemed drunk to the
onlookers. 'For goodness sake,' Peter must have thought,
for he makes reference to it later, 'it's only nine o'clock in
the morning. Too early for folk to be drunk. Anyway, the
insinuation prompted Peter to deliver 'the first sermon',
a fundamental presentation of the gospel. The reader will
have noticed that we have gone beyond the gospels to the
Acts to get a final perspective on the story of Jesus. The
passage which follows is weighed down with meaning
and richness. However, we will just mention a few points
that serve the purpose of this volume. Peter points out
that the high spirits of the disciples are signs of the fulfil-*

ment of the Old Testament prophecy of Joel as to what is to happen 'in the last days'. The linking of the present to the Old Testament is significant in showing the continuity of things. Peter then turns his attention to what God has done in Jesus and gives a summary of his wonderful works, his crucifixion and resurrection, culminating in scriptural evidence that he is the Lord and Messiah. Peter speaks directly of Jesus here; Jesus never spoke directly about himself. His great concern was the kingdom. Peter, and later Paul and other early preachers, focused directly on Jesus. It was as if they could not speak of the kingdom until they had dealt with the figure of Christ. The message became focused on the risen Jesus as Messiah and Son of God (cf Romans 1:3-4). What emerges is that Jesus is the piece that gives meaning to the whole plan of God. In the passage, we also witness conversions and baptisms. This aspect we will take up in the final session.

14But Peter, standing with the eleven, raised his voice and addressed them, 'Men of Judea and all who live in Jerusalem, let this be known to you, and listen to what I say. 15Indeed these are not drunk, as you suppose, for it is only nine o'clock in the morning. 16No, this is what was spoken through the prophet Joel:

17"In the last days it will be, God declares, that I will pour out my Spirit upon all flesh, and your sons and your daughters shall prophesy, and your young men shall see visions, and your old men shall dream dreams.

18Even upon my slaves, both men and women, in those days I will pour out my Spirit; and they shall prophesy.

19And I will show portents in the heaven above and signs on the earth below, blood, and fire, and smoky mist.

20The sun shall be turned to darkness and the moon

to blood, before the coming of the Lord's great and glorious day.

21Then everyone who calls on the name of the Lord shall be saved."

22'You that are Israelites, listen to what I have to say: Jesus of Nazareth, a man attested to you by God with deeds of power, wonders, and signs that God did through him among you, as you yourselves know – 23this man, handed over to you according to the definite plan and foreknowledge of God, you crucified and killed by the hands of those outside the law. 24But God raised him up, having freed him from death, because it was impossible for him to be held in its power. 25For David says concerning him, "I saw the Lord always before me, for he is at my right hand so that I will not be shaken; 26therefore my heart was glad, and my tongue rejoiced; moreover my flesh will live in hope. 27For you will not abandon my soul to Hades, or let your Holy One experience corruption. 28You have made known to me the ways of life; you will make me full of gladness with your presence."

29'Fellow Israelites, I may say to you confidently of our ancestor David that he both died and was buried, and his tomb is with us to this day. 30Since he was a prophet, he knew that God had sworn an oath to him that he would put one of his descendants on his throne. 31Foreseeing this, David spoke of the resurrection of the Messiah, saying, "He was not abandoned to Hades, nor did his flesh experience corruption."

32This Jesus God raised up, and of that all of us are witnesses. 33Being therefore exalted at the right hand of God, and having received from the Father the promise of the Holy Spirit, he has poured out this that you both see and hear. 34For David did not ascend into heaven, but he himself says, "The Lord said to my

Lord, 'Sit on my right hand, [35]until I make your enemies your footstool.'"

[36]Therefore let the entire house of Israel know with certainty that God has made him both Lord and Messiah, this Jesus whom you crucified.'

[37]Now when they had heard this, they were cut to the heart and said to Peter and the other apostles, 'Brothers what should we do?' [38]Peter said to them, 'Repent and be baptised every one of you in the name of Jesus Christ so that your sins may be forgiven; and you will receive the gift of the Holy Spirit. [39]For the promise is for you, for your children, and for all who are far away, everyone whom the Lord our God calls to him.' [40]And he testified with many other arguments and exhorted them, saying, 'Save yourself from this corrupt generation.' [41]So those who welcomed his message were baptised, and that day about three thousand persons were added. [42]They devoted themselves to the apostles' teaching, and fellowship, to the breaking of bread and prayers.

Questions
1) What do you learn about Jesus from the foregoing passage?
2) What impressed, questioned, or challenged you in the extract?
3) Taking your personal experience of Christ into account, does the passage strike any intimate chords for you? *(Because of the nature of this question, it is provided for personal rather than group reflection.)*

Reality/Action
How do we put the word of God we have heard into practice? Is there something we can do? Or are we doing something that can be done better? Are there

attitudes to change? *(The group should decide on some practical outcome.)*

Spontaneous Prayer

1) Merciful Lord, grant that we never forget all that you have done for us through your Son, Our Lord Jesus Christ. Lord hear us.

R. Lord graciously hear us.

2) Hidden God, how endearing is the Jesus who is reluctant to speak directly of himself. May we capture something of his humility and self-effacement. Lord hear us.

R. Lord graciously hear us.

3) Lord, help us to give witness to the risen Jesus as Messiah and Son of God. Lord hear us.

R. Lord graciously hear us.

The participants may now add their own prayers and petitions. When these prayers and petitions end, there is the recitation of:

The Lord's Prayer

Blessing

May the God of our Saviour be blessed.

R. Amen

May the Son be glorified.

R. Amen.

May the Spirit be heeded.

R. Amen.

And may almighty God bless you, the Father, the Son, and the Holy Spirit.

R. Amen.

Hymn
An appropriate hymn may be sung.

Session 33
Christ emerging in history

Opening Prayer
Lord, we place ourselves in your presence. Send us your
Spirit to enlighten our minds and open our hearts to
your word. We know that Jesus is with us because we
are gathered in his name, and he tells us '... where two
or three are gathered in my name. I am with them.'
We also invite our holy mother Mary, the Seat of
Wisdom, to be part of our sharing. Amen.

Scripture Sharing (Ephesians 4:14-16)
This passage is most revealing of Christ from a perspective
beyond the gospels, as Christians tease out in history what
his life means. In the opening prayer of each session in this
volume we have the words of Jesus, 'For where two or
three are gathered in my name, I am with them'
(Matthew 18:20). The following extract provides a
superb development of that truth. We are the body of
Christ (cf 1 Corinthians 12:27). Christ is the head of
that body, we are the body knit together by every liga-
ment. The risen Christ lives in us in a real way. People
sometimes say, 'Che lives!' or 'Mahatma lives!' but they
don't. They are dead and turned to dust. Their memories
may live, or their influence, yet not themselves. The risen
Christ, however, has conquered death and truly lives. He
is still with us. For us it remains to grow into the stature
of Christ and help build his body up in love. Historically,
it was felt that some folk had a special role in this body:
the clergy were sometimes considered the neck of the body,
mediating with Jesus the head and with the Godhead on
behalf of the rest. Not so! We (I am a cleric) are parts of
the body like the remainder of God's 'priestly people'. And
there is only one mediator between God and humans,

and that is Christ the Lord. In the early church this was borne out by the way all the faithful partook in the liturgy. All were actively involved, not as a nine days wonder, rather as normal procedure (cf 1 Corinthians 14:26-33). Verse 26 of this passage just cited from 1 Corinthians says: 'When you come together, each one has a hymn, a lesson, a revelation, a tongue, or an interpretation.' The Greek word used for 'when' – (h)otan – carries the connotation 'whenever' rather than an isolated 'when'. So the normal procedure involved full participation by all the people of God. And so we see that the story of Jesus grows in history and will do so as long as this world lasts.

14We must no longer be children, tossed to and fro and blown about by every wind of doctrine, by people's trickery, by their craftiness in deceitful scheming. 15But speaking the truth in love, we must grow up in every way into him who is the head, into Christ, 16from whom the whole body, joined and knit together by every ligament with which it is equipped, as each part is working properly, promotes the body's growth in building itself up in love.

Questions

1) What do you learn about Jesus from the foregoing passage?

2) What impressed, questioned, or challenged you in the extract?

3) Taking your personal experience of Christ into account, does the passage strike any intimate chords for you? *(Because of the nature of this question, it is provided for personal rather than group reflection.)*

Reality/Action

How do we put the word of God we have heard into practice? Is there something we can do? Or are we doing something that can be done better? Are there attitudes to change? *(The group should decide on some practical outcome.)*

Spontaneous Prayer
1) God of unity, grant that we grow into the stature of Christ, the head, and in so doing build up the body of Christ in love. Lord hear us.
R. Lord graciously hear us.
2) God in whom there is no deceit, help us to follow him who is the way, the truth, and the life by always speaking the truth in love. Lord hear us.
R. Lord graciously hear us.
3) Lord, help all clerics not to exaggerate their role in the body of Christ. Lord hear us.
R. Lord graciously hear us.
The participants may now add their own prayers and petitions. When these prayers and petitions end, there is the recitation of:
The Lord's Prayer

Blessing
May we not be tossed to and fro.
R. Amen,
May we speak the truth in love.
R. Amen.
May we grow into the stature of Christ.
R. Amen.
And may almighty God bless you, the Father, the Son, and the Holy Spirit.
R. Amen.

Hymn
An appropriate hymn may be sung.

Epilogue

And so our search for Christ from a selection of key scripture readings (gospel mainly) is ended. We are, hopefully, even greater and more intimate friends with him as a result. But the search is a never ending one, for the whole Bible is essentially about Christ. The Old Testament prepares for and anticipates his life, a life that becomes reality in the New Testament, and the remainder of the Bible teases out its consequences. We may even feel motivated to read the whole Bible at least once, as many people do. This can be achieved by beginning at the beginning and ploughing through methodically to the end, which could become an endurance test. Best to have some strategy. A friend and scripture scholar, Carlo Buzzetti, once told me that a useful approach to this mammoth task would be to start from the Acts of the Apostles and work one's way through those. When the Acts give references to other parts of the Bible, one should go to these at a convenient point and read them too. In this way one could get to the heart of the Bible. Other methods are suggested in the appendices of Bibles. In these appendices passages suitable for various occasions are also given. The Good News Gospel, for example, which has separate booklets for Matthew, Mark, and Luke do this; again the Gideon Bible does so. Anyway, I hope the readers' interest in, and contact with, the word of God will continue always.

Appendix
Method for reflection on any Bible passage

1) Invite those present to place themselves in the presence of God (pause in silence).

2) Ask for a volunteer to read the passage and leave a couple of minutes for the members to think about it. Do not fear the silence; it gives the Spirit a chance to speak.

3) Read the extract a second time (different reader) and pause once more for three to five minutes.

4) Invite the participants to share regarding what the passage says to them, paying particular attention to how it impresses, questions, or challenges them.

5) Determine the practical application of the passage. How do they put the word of God they have heard into practice? Is there something they can do? Are they doing something that can be done better? Are there attitudes to change? The group should decide on some practical outcome.

6) Shared Prayer (cf this feature in the meetings of this volume).

Note: If, before the reading, a brief and simple introduction to the passage could be given or read, it would be helpful.

By the same author
The Brendan Book of Prayer
for small groups/couples
(may be used by individuals)

'The commentaries on the Gospel passages, simply, yet profoundly written ... fresh insights into Jesus and the Gospel story. A good book for personal reflection and for the busy homilist.'   – Donal Neary SJ, *The Furrow*, Ireland.

'Excellent ... a lovely little volume to hold. The author's preface and poem in honour of Brendan the Navigator and the appealing cover design won this reviewer over from the outset.'   – Brian Power, *Books Ireland.*

'A wonderful book, beautifully produced, beautifully written. There should be one in every home.'
   – Gerry Glennon, *Mid and North-west Radios,* Ireland.

'Well worth reading' – *Link Up,* Dublin.

'A very fine little book which all groups will find inspiring.'
   – Books Editor, *The Irish Catholic.*

Available from your usual supplier or direct from:
The Columba Press,
55A Spruce Avenue, Stillorgan Industrial Park,
Blackrock, Co Dublin, Ireland.
E-mail: sales@columba.ie
(available in Australia, New Zealand, the United States, Canada)

Also available, by O'Halloran, from same sources
• *When the Acacia Bird Sings* (novel)
• *Remember José Inga!* (novel, Spring 2004)
• *The Least of These* (short stories)

By the same author

Small Christian Communities
Vision and Practicalities

Latest revision and update of this book of which it has been said:

'At last the book I have longed to see from the person best fitted to write it. Whatever the form of ministry, lay or ordained, I was able to recommend this major work as one filled with wisdom. For me this is the Book of the Year, a treasure and a treasure trove.'
— Dr Ian Fraser, *Coracle,* Iona, Scotland.

'Very useful to pastors, ministers and parish councils...much of value to say. In a work packed with theological, psychological and scriptural insights he has succeeded in being surprisingly methodical.   —Brian Power, *Books Ireland.*

'One of the best introductions to small Christian communities.'   — Margaret Hebblethwaite, *The Tablet,* England.

'Clear about the elements of a viable ecclesial vision for the 21st Century.'
— Dennis Geaney, *National Catholic Reporter,* USA.

'Anyone seeking a vision of a renewed Church should read this book. A text of unimpeachable quality.'
— Liam S. Maher, *Hallel,* Europe.

Available from your usual supplier or direct from:
The Columba Press,
55A Spruce Avenue, Stillorgan Industrial Park,
Blackrock, Co. Dublin, Ireland.
E-mail: sales@columba.ie
(available in Australia, New Zealand, the United States, Canada)